REA

Stevenson
and Victorian Scotland

Stevenson and Victorian Scotland

EDITED BY JENNI CALDER

at the University Press
EDINBURGH

★

© Edinburgh University Press
and individual contributors 1981
22 George Square, Edinburgh

ISBN 0 85224 399 5

Printed in Great Britain by
Redwood Burn Limited
Trowbridge & Esher

Contents

2227364

JENNI CALDER

Introduction
Stevenson in Perspective

Robert Louis Stevenson has been one of the most elusive writers in
the English language. Conventional critical approaches generally
look for a degree of categorisation: to feel comfortable with an
author a label is considered necessary. The description on the label
may be modified, proved to be inadequate, extended, but the label
itself, implicitly indicating how we should read an author, remains
accepted practice. Stevenson is a writer with whom most of us
profess to feel comfortable. We think we know him. Yet he has
elicited a variety of evasive responses from serious readers; coy
praise, effusive keenness, puzzled irritation, reluctant acknow-
ledgement. And even in the case of praise and enthusiasm there has
often been a dismissive element, which has come sometimes from
those who have been content to accept his curious, tributary position in British literature without much enquiry.

Does Stevenson fit into a Scottish, an English, a European, or an
American tradition? Although in the forefront of Scottish literature, he was involved, and had much in common, with English
writers of his generation, and looked to the south for his orienta-
tion. Yet he had a knowledge of French writers and was greatly
influenced by them, feeling more of a cultural affinity with France
than he did with England, which he found, in many respects, alien
territory. He was certainly more at home in France than in England,
and possibly than he was in Scotland. His relationship with America was crucial. He had a vigorous admiration for certain American
writers, for Whitman and Hawthorne, for instance. America re-
sponded with enthusiasm for his own work which Britain did not
match, and was prepared to back him with hard cash. His marriage
to an American was no accident. Fanny Osbourne had qualities that
Stevenson admired in American life and literature: independence,
toughness and unconventionality. Stevenson is an international

writer in more than the sense that, like Burns and Scott, his
companions in an uneasy triad, he has been translated into many
languages and has been seen to have something to say to many
cultures. He has an internationalism that Burns and Scott lack, a
responsiveness to multiple traditions, a gift not only for language
and languages but for variations in cultural and psychological
nuances. Looked at in the light of his French or American or Pacific
experiences, for instance, we may begin to wonder what he is doing
in the position of officially acknowledged (though some would
argue not sufficiently acknowledged) great Scottish writer. Yet he
is as directly a product of Scotland, and of Victorian Scotland, as it
was possible to be. By looking at Stevenson the man and Stevenson
the writer we can learn a great deal about his place and his time, and
about that profound Scottish need, which perhaps came to a climax
in the nineteenth century, to seek somewhere else.

Since the 1880s lip-service has been paid to Stevenson's achievement, even by those who, as Professor Harvie indicates, were
privately unimpressed. Adulation of the man has deflected critical
attention from his work. Enthusiasm for a handful of his books –
Travels with a Donkey, Treasure Island – has made it easier to
neglect a substantial amount of his writing. His secure position in
the Scottish canon has meant a certain lack of concern for areas
where he moved outside Scottish territory. Stevenson not only had
a mercurial personality, he has left a mercurial legacy for twentieth-
century readers. An inquisitive reading of Stevenson still has much
to uncover. It was this implicit challenge that lay behind the symposium on 'Robert Louis Stevenson and Victorian Scotland' that
was held in Edinburgh in July 1980, and which has produced this
book.

The symposium proved to be a major step in a fresh exploration
of Stevenson. It brought together those who have been rather
lonely pioneers in Stevenson studies, those who have long derived
pleasure from his writing, and those who have quite recently
turned their attention to his work. Perhaps what emerged most
strikingly from this gathering was that Stevenson remains a writer
who continually challenges and tantalises. He was a man of fluid
mind and temperament, with a heart and an intellect of sparkling
attentiveness. This combined with his concern to get things right,
a deeply moral honesty, is a radical aspect of his writing's character.

Some of his contemporaries noted that he lacked rigorous intellectual application; J. A. Symonds was one who was troubled by
this, commenting on it in a somewhat patronising way. It is true

that Stevenson worked best in a situation of immediacy, whether of an idea, a feeling, a particular interest or an enthusiasm, and when the immediacy faded he was in trouble. This dependence on immediate stimulus was part of the explanation for his problems in sustaining a lengthy narrative. We know it interfered with, for instance, *Treasure Island* and *The Master of Ballantrae*, and possibly accounts for the rather abrupt, but surely effective, ending of *Kidnapped*. But if the fading of immediacy caused problems in his writing there were certain things that Stevenson was able to keep alive with extraordinary vividness: his childhood, his experiences of Edinburgh as he was growing up, and perhaps most incontrovertibly of all his sense of Scotland during his final years in the South Pacific.

This gift fed his best writing. But it also highlights certain things that he had difficulty with – his own personality, for instance. He could not recapture in prose the quicksilver qualities of his own conversation, the rapid movements of his mind, the delicacy and depth of his emotional responses – except in his letters. In fact, he believed that he should not try. One of his hardest tasks as a writer must have been to discipline his lightning personality. Yet there are moments when his own delight in an experience, an idea, a scene or a memory or a tone of voice lends a quite independent life to his language. They can be found in some of the pieces on his childhood, for example in 'The Lantern Bearers', in the language of *Weir of Hermiston*'s elder Kirstie, in *Edinburgh: Picturesque Notes*, moments when self and craft coalesce.

This at once suggests one of the main problems of an approach to Stevenson. It is well known that he is artful. His prose has been both praised and condemned on those grounds. Stevenson the self-conscious craftsman has caused much concern. *Travels with a Donkey* is a good example of a carefully crafted book, often regarded as a minor masterpiece, widely enjoyed, which in fact has very little to say – and which is at its best just at that point where he has most to *tell*, when Stevenson is discussing the Camisards, so close to the Covenanters who rode his mind so fiercely. In that chapter his language becomes taut and fully engaged. Elsewhere its very accuracy can be dull. *Travels with a Donkey* is praised because it is a pleasing account of R.L.S. adventuring with a donkey through the wild and evocative country of the Cévennes. But is it? Is it not rather an evasion of R.L.S., the mind and feelings of the man during that autumn of 1878, when the woman he loved had returned to her husband six thousand miles away and Scotland seemed to have little to offer? There are moments when the book has a pedestrian quality that matches the pedestrian nature of the journey. Modestine is, surely, a distraction, and at times a tedious one, from the man. The man has developed an attractively quirky literary persona which protects the real self from exposure. And it was this that he was working at when he played the sedulous ape, the development of a workable literary persona via an appropriate style, rather than style itself, during his early apprenticeship years. The early Stevenson has a guarded fluency. He writes about himself as if he were someone else – 'Ordered South' illustrates the polite detachment of self from subject where we *know* he is writing about himself and that every word is informed by painful experience. Yet the demands of style, of the etiquette of style, are that language must be so finely distilled that the original robust ingredients cannot be detected.

It would be misleading to labour this point, for the larger part of Stevenson's literary career is taken up by a process away from this. Within that process, its personal and literary circumstances, its context and its results, lies all the fascination of Robert Louis Stevenson. As the essays collected here show he was a man irrevocably shaped by his Scottish Calvinist background, but also by the wider social and cultural environment of the second half of the century. Stevenson was the son of the first established generation of the professional middle class. He came to maturity in the decade, the 1870s, in which we can detect major cultural turning points. In literature the Victorian giants of the novel were dead or nearly so, and fiction and attitudes towards it were changing. Stevenson himself was much involved in the reaction against naturalism, which he felt had deadened fiction. The 1870s saw the first exhibitions of Impressionist paintings. Stevenson spent a great deal of time in France in the 1870s, and took a close interest in the work of the younger generation of painters, and in the debate about realism in art. When he came to write about realism in fiction, in 'A Humble Remonstrance', analogies with painting were useful to him.

Stevenson's intimate involvement with these changes of focus, attitude and expectation suggest that we can look at him usefully almost as a case history of their influences, although neither as personality nor writer does he quite seem to fit in with anyone else. His growing up in Scotland, within a distinct tradition and at a distance from London, the place that was regarded by many as the literary capital of the world, intensifies but does not alter this aspect of Stevenson. His reaction to established religion, for example, is more acute for the strict Calvinism of his upbringing and the painful religious commitment of his father. His efforts to move out of the range of middle-class morality are more powerful owing to his upbringing in Edinburgh's New Town, an area created by and for the successful middle and upper classes, deeply imprinted with values that Stevenson's generation saw were failing to cope with realities. His commitment to writing is more significant when set in a moral and religious environment that regarded the imagination and the gratifications of art with the greatest suspicion.

Many of Stevenson's generation were involved in these reactions. The profound disturbance precipitated by Darwin in 1856, after a century or so of rumbling, was a symptom of the painful legacies of a generation that had striven to control the combined forces of humanity and technology. At the same time that men and women were discovering that the world was a much more complicated place than had ever been thought, and that humanity's place in it was not as incontrovertible as previous mythical and intellectual constructs had suggested, immediate exigencies seem to demand more rigid controls, more limited definitions of behaviour. Stevenson's generation was inclined to react simultaneously both anarchistically and with an energetic brand of moral and political Toryism. Stevenson himself reveals a teasing mixture of the Tory and the radical. He was acutely aware of what could happen when moral structures collapsed, he wrote about this often, but he made it quite clear that the individual had to work out his own code of behaviour, his own morality. A blind adherence to someone else's set of rules was worthless, even dangerous. Areas of responsibility had to be defined independently. This is territory that Stevenson explores in his essays, in stories and in his novels. If his work contains a single overall message, which can be found lurking in *Treasure Island*, in *Prince Otto*, in *Dr Jekyll and Mr Hyde*, in many of his poems and most acutely in the work of the last five years of his life, it is this. It is a message about individual moral responsibility.

The general effect of life, of experience and of the rules that attempt to control it are, Stevenson felt, deadening. 'Our attention requires to be surprised', he writes in *Lay Morals*, and he says the same kind of thing in a number of places.[1] In *Lay Morals* Stevenson is talking specifically about the Bible, about how it had 'lost its message for the common run of hearers'. But overall he is saying that life itself has lost its message, that literature has lost its message, and it is this that he wants to do something about. To regain a sense of surprise and delight in experience an alertness is necessary, and a shedding of the moral and cultural padding that stands between humanity and life. In a number of ways the reaction to bourgeois Victorianism implies this: radicalism, anarchy, a preoccupation with language, texture, colour with an apparent disregard for moral structure. Again we are confronted with the challenge of Stevenson. His regard for moral structure is deep and insistent, yet he aimed for a finely wrought language. His early concern for style perhaps makes more sense if it can be explained as developing into a profound interest in bringing life and language as close together as possible. The artificialities that operate in his efforts to create a convincing and appropriate persona are worn away as experience and maturity have their inevitable effect.

Stevenson had a profound understanding of the potential of language. There is nothing fortuitous about his strengths as a writer. Yet it is possible that this understanding and his acute sensitivity towards words and their power interfered with his development. His problem was twofold: to evolve a language that could bring together personality and subject, so that he could write directly of experience and his own place in experience. We can see this development at work if we turn from *Travels with a Donkey* to *An Amateur Emigrant*. And to produce an effective narrative language, that would again take him within his subject and provide the range and pace that he required. This aspect of the problem he solved sporadically. He certainly solved it in *Kidnapped*, in many of the short stories, partially overcame it in *The Ebb Tide*, for large parts of *The Master of Ballantrae*. I am not convinced that Stevenson solved it in *Weir of Hermiston*, and I feel that its being unfinished is of considerable importance in any argument about its achievement.

Stevenson worked closely from experience, both first and second hand. The 'personal' ingredient in his writing comes not only from the need to control or come to terms with his own personality, but also from the way he nourished his writing so directly from life. The two things are of course connected and suggest another complicating factor in any attempt to place Stevenson, for this intimacy with experience does not seem compatible with his reputation as a romancist. The strengths of Stevenson's imagination are generally acknowledged. But it was an imagination that was as much, if not more, transforming than inventive. It worked richly on what there was to hand, and he deliberately sought out stimulating material with which to feed it. He had no interest, or for a long time thought he had not, in a Zolaesque accurate recording of reality, but the nature of reality is nevertheless fundamental to his writing. He said himself in 'A Humble Remonstrance' that the art of the novelist was 'occupied, not so much in making stories true as in making them typical'.[2] And he would have agreed with his contemporary Hardy that 'a novel is an impression, not an argument'.[3] Nevertheless the imagination itself can furnish a message, a moral, can lead as strongly as didacticism. We only have to look at what Stevenson chose to write about, particularly in his last years, to realise how insistently he sought, in life, the right kind of material. The years in the Pacific were a crucial part of this search, not just an accident of ill health or a dreamer's search for escape.

We can see the transforming imagination at work in the fiction Stevenson produced in these last years, and we can see too how by approaching his material more directly and not seeking to shelter behind a careful construct of polished expression he was solving the problems of language and narrative. A passage from *The Ebb Tide*, a neglected novel, is illustrative:

> The old calaboose, in which the waifs had so long harboured, is a low, rectangular enclosure of building at the corner of a shady western avenue and a little townward of the British consulate. Within was a grassy court, littered with wreckage and the traces of vagrant occupation. Six or seven cells opened from the court: the doors, that had once been locked on mutinous whalermen, rotting before them in the grass. No mark remained of their old destination, except the rusty bars upon the windows.
>
> The floor of one of the cells had been a little cleared; a bucket (the last remaining piece of furniture of the three caitiffs) stood full of water by the door, a half cocoanut shell beside it for a drinking-cup; and on some ragged ends of mat Huish sprawled asleep, his mouth open, his face deathly. The glow of the tropic afternoon, the green of sunbright foliage, stared into that shady place through door and window; and Herrick, pacing to and fro on the coral floor, sometimes paused and laved his face and neck with tepid water from the bucket. His long arrears of suffering, the night's vigil, the insults of the morning, and the harrowing business of the letter, had strung him to the point when pain is almost a pleasure, time shrinks to a mere point, and death and life appear indifferent. To and fro he paced like a caged brute; his mind whirling through the universe of thought and memory; his eyes, as he

went, skimming the legends on the wall. The crumbling
whitewash was full of them: Tahitian names, and French, and
English, and rude sketches of ships under sail and men at
fisticuffs.[4]

We know that Stevenson had walked the beach at Papeete and had
seen the old calaboose that he is describing here. Like so much of
what he observed in the Pacific the scene was highly suggestive.
Adventuring from island to island had, anyway, an immediacy that
often seemed more than real. And Stevenson could separate himself from what he saw in a way that he could not in the case of
Scotland, and Edinburgh in particular. In the Pacific his feelings
were certainly engaged, but they were not rooted.

The old calaboose appears as Stevenson saw it. He introduces the
characters that the environment and circumstances of Papeete, the
seedy result of the impact of third-rate and second-hand European
civilisation on native Tahiti, invite. His description is precise. The
precision extends to character as well as place. There is a feeling for
composition here, a suggestion of a genre painting: the contrast of
sun and shade, the impressionistic glow and the definition of
objects – the bucket and coconut shell, Huish sprawled asleep, the
graffiti on the wall, Herrick pacing up and down. Yet the sugges-
tiveness is much wider than the usual inwardness and self-contain-
ment of a genre interior. Stevenson was always sensitive to the
presence of ghosts, of spirits out of the past, half-tangible links
with other places, other times. There are ghosts here too. They are
not just the ghosts of mutinous whalermen or of South Sea beach-
combers or the presence of Melville and his *Omoo*, but spirits of the
civilisation Herrick both forces himself to remember and cannot
ever forget, however painful its haunting. In the following paragraph he scratches the opening bars of Beethoven's Fifth Sym-
phony on the calaboose wall, to add his own imprint to those of the
long gone, and remembers scraps of Horace and Virgil.

There are times when Stevenson writes about Scotland, perhaps
especially in *Weir of Hermiston*, when his awareness of the force of
emotive meaning contained in the places and scenes and the kinds
of people he describes tempts him to strain to match it with his
language. This does not happen here. The intrinsic drama is mu-
ted. Much of *The Ebb Tide* is close to melodrama, but the elements
that we might expect to be elaborated at the hands of the romancist
are allowed to make their own impact. The account has a neutral
and objective quality, coloured by Herrick's misery, which throws
into relief the extreme situation of the three central characters

without the need for an extra effort at dramatisation. The passage quoted does contain some characteristic peculiarities : the deliberate archaism 'caitiff', for instance, the slightly coy 'waif', the slightly ponderous 'long arrears of suffering', the perhaps exaggerated 'whirling through the universe of thought and memory'. Yet, looked at again, it can be seen they have their own exactness. There is no doubt that they are the words that Stevenson wished to use, and if they jar a little, it is because of the jarring nature of the collision that *The Ebb Tide* is all about, the collision of cultures, which has the effect of destroying the essential props of both.

This brings only briefly into focus some of the problems of language and style that account in part for the evasive criticial reactions that Stevenson's work has generated for over a century. Ultimately, before a complete assessment of his achievement can be made, this will have to be explored more closely. Stevenson cared profoundly about the use of language and about the potential of fiction. He never doubted the value of story-telling. This concern was heightened by his Calvinist background. Calvinism not only saw the workings of the imagination as an indulgence but relied heavily on the power of words, the emotive qualities of language, to communicate an awareness of sin and commitment. Brought up on the Old Testament, on tales of the Covenanting martyrs, and on ingredients of a profound folk tradition Stevenson could scarcely have avoided being intensely aware of the force of language over human behaviour and belief. His concern for both language and fiction had a great deal to do with his understanding that words were to be respected as well as mastered. His careful crafting of style stemmed from this too. Even his letters, so often spontaneous, unrestrained, apparently careless sometimes, show his sensitivity towards words, and his respect for them is clear.

Stevenson's style cannot be separated from his life or his background just as his choice of subject must be seen also in this context. There is perhaps no other writer in the English language for whom this is more true. It is impossible for the critic to withdraw from the details of the man's life, and impossible to understand the man's personality and actions if his writing is ignored. It is appropriate, then, that this book ranges through both. The wider context of his life and work is established, and some of the most pertinent details of his development filled in. Two essays specifically concentrate on his fiction – and if one area is selected in which his reputation is most likely to be sustained it is his fiction.

What about that reputation? It has suffered considerably from over-enthusiasm and an uncritical hero-worship. It has suffered equally from a kind of negative acceptance of his value. It has suffered from the swithering attitudes towards his life, from the early attempts to distract attention from the less palatable aspects, to the subsequent efforts to romanticise his bohemianism. In spite of the work of a number of writers and critics, most notably J. C. Furnas and David Daiches, vestiges of these attitudes remain, not so much in the way his life is now seen as in the way his work is approached, or not approched. W. W. Robson wonders, in his essay on *Kidnapped*, why Leavis did not include Stevenson in his 'great tradition'. The answer may be that he simply forgot him. Although the exclusion of the reinstated Dickens, for instance, requires some explanation, however brief, most critics, even now, would probably not feel obliged to justify the exclusion of Stevenson from the nineteenth-century canon. (It is curious that one can most confidently expect to find Stevenson represented in collections of nineteenth-century verse, and although he wrote a number of skilled and very moving poems few would make extravagant claims for his achievement as a poet.) Much of Stevenson's most interesting work is out of print, so there is an immediate disincentive for the less than highly motivated to read him. It requires prolonged hunting through the second-hand book shops or long sessions in the libraries. Availability accounts for a great deal.

There is no danger that Stevenson will be forgotten. But he may be remembered totally out-of-focus. Or he may continue to be not so much forgotten as left in some backwater of the literary critical mind, becalmed like one of his own pirate ships, awaiting some freshening breeze of interest. We hope that this book and the events that have surrounded its production, two exhibitions on his life and work in the summer of 1980, the accompanying symposium, a refurbished Stevenson museum in his native city, and the inauguration of a new collected edition of his work, will provide some impetus towards setting the reading of Stevenson on course again.

References
1   'Lay Morals', Collected Works (Skerryvore Edition) vol. XXII, 165.
2   'A Humble Remonstrance', ibid., vol. XXV, 159.
3   Thomas Hardy, *Tess of the D'Urbervilles* (Macmillan 1967) introduction, vii.
4   *The Ebb Tide*, Collected Works (Skerryvore Edition) vol. X, 227.

DAVID DAICHES

Stevenson and Scotland

In July 1879 Stevenson was working on his essay about Burns for
the *Cornhill*. On the 24th he wrote from Swanston to Edmund
Gosse discussing the poet:

> I am sorry to say it, but there was something in him of the
> vulgar, bagmanlike, professional seducer. – Oblige me by
> taking down and reading, for the hundredth time I hope, his
> *Twa Dogs* and his *Address to the Unco Guid*. I am only a
> Scotchman, after all, you see; and when I have beaten Burns, I
> am driven at once, by my parental feelings, to console him
> with a sugar-plum. But hang me if I know anything I like so
> well as the *Twa Dogs*. Even a common Englishman may have a
> glimpse, as it were from Pisgah, of its extraordinary merits.
> '*English, The:* – a dull people, incapable of comprehending the
> Scottish tongue. Their history is so intimately connected with
> that of Scotland, that we must refer our readers to that heading.
> Their literature is principally the work of venal Scots.'
> – Stevenson's *Handy Cyclopaedia*. Glescow: Blaikie &
> Bannock.[1]

The mixture of pride and mockery, of admiration and depreca-
tion, is characteristic of Stevenson's attitude towards his native
country. He loved Scotland and deeply felt his roots as a Scot. In the
last months of his life he was writing both to Charles Baxter and to
his cousin Bob Stevenson about his ancestry. In September 1893 he
wrote to Baxter about a seventeenth-century James Stevenson of
Nether-Carswell in the parish of Neilston and asked him 'to com-
pulse the parish registers of Neilston, if they exist, and go back so
far'. He exclaimed in mock-triumph: 'Can I have really found the
tap-root of my illustrious ancestry at last?'[2] In June 1894 he wrote in
a less ambiguous tone to Bob Stevenson, claiming that he was both
'Cymry and Pict'. He added: 'We may have fought with King Arthur

and known Merlin. The first of the family, Stevenson of Stevenson, was quite a great party, and dates back to the wars of Edward First.' On his mother's side he had already (in his essay 'The Manse', recollections of childhood play in his maternal grandfather's house, which appeared in *Scribner's* in 1887) claimed adventurous Border ancestry: 'I have shaken a spear in the Debateable Land and shouted the slogan of the Elliots.' He went back to this side of his ancestry in drawing the elder Kirstie in his unfinished masterpiece, *Weir of Hermiston*.

The urge to escape from Scotland was no less potent in him than the urge to seek his roots there. This point emerges very clearly from the opening of *Edinburgh: Picturesque Notes*:

> The ancient and famous metropolis of the North sits overlooking a windy estuary from the slope and summit of three hills. No situation could be more commanding for the head city of a kingdom; none better chosen for noble prospects. From her tall precipice and terraced gardens she looks far and wide on the sea and broad champaigns. To the east you may catch at sunset the spark of the May lighthouse, where the Firth expands into the German Ocean; and away to the west, over all the carse of Stirling, you can see the first snows upon Ben Ledi.
>
> But Edinburgh pays cruelly for her high seat in one of the vilest climates under heaven. She is liable to be beaten upon by all the winds that blow, to be drenched with rain, to be buried in cold sea fogs out of the east, and powdered with snow as it comes flying southward from the Highland hills. The weather is raw and boisterous in winter, shifty and ungenial in summer, and a downright necrological purgatory in the spring. . . . For all who love shelter and the blessings of the sun, who hate dark weather and perpetual tilting against squalls, there could scarcely be found a more unhomely and harassing place of residence. Many such aspire angrily after that Somewhere-else of the imagination, where all troubles are supposed to end. They lean over the great bridge which joins the New Town with the Old – that windiest spot, or high altar, in this northern temple of the winds – and watch the trains smoking out from under them and vanishing into the tunnel on a voyage to brighter skies. Happy the passengers who shake off the dust of Edinburgh, and have heard for the last time the cry of the east wind among her chimney-tops! And yet the place establishes an interest in people's hearts; go where they will, they find no

city of the same distinction; go where they will, they take a
pride in their old home.[3]

It is all there, put quite dramatically in his picture of his native
city: love and pride on the one hand, desperate desire to escape on
the other.

The climate (which seems to have been worse in Stevenson's
childhood than it was in my childhood in Edinburgh, when the
prevailing wind was south-westerly and the summers at least were
warm) and his own precarious health were of course significant
factors in creating this desire to escape, although, as we shall see,
there were other equally important factors at work. The sickly boy,
confined to the Land of Counterpane, obsessed with the wind
howling down the chimney and encircling the house like a furious
aerial horseman, imagining escape and adventure from the security
of his comfortable middle-class home – it is all in *A Child's Garden
of Verses*. In his late thirties he remembered how it felt to be a boy
longing for adventure yet at the same time anticipating a return to
the familiar scenes of childhood after all the adventures were over:

Over the borders, a sin without pardon,
  Breaking the branches and crawling below,
Out through the breach in the wall of the garden,
  Down by the banks of the river, we go. . . .

Home from the Indies and home from the ocean,
  Heroes and soldiers we all shall come home;
Still we shall find the old mill wheel in motion,
  Turning and churning the river to foam.

You with the bean that I gave when we quarrelled,
  I with your marble of Saturday last,
Honoured and old and all gaily apparelled,
  Here we shall meet and remember the past.[4]

'Here we shall meet and remember the past.' This is a remarkable
example of nostalgia *anticipated* in childhood, when the child is
still in a present that is to become a past that will evoke nostalgia. It
shows how strong the nostalgic theme was in Stevenson, the
compulsive exile and lover of home. His letters to Charles Baxter
are liable to continuous flooding with nostalgia, from quite an early
age. Here he is writing to Baxter from France in early July 1877:

For making all allowance for little rubs and hitches, the past
looks very delightful to me: the past when you were not going
to be married, and I was not trying to write a novel; the past
when you went through to B of Allan to contemplate Mrs.

Chawles in the house of God, and I went home trembling every
day lest Heaven should open and the thunderbolt of parental
anger light upon my head; the past where we have been drunk
and sober, and sat outside of grocers' shops on fine dark
nights, and wrangled in the Speculative, and heard mysterious
whistling in Waterloo Place, and met missionaries from Aber-
deen; generally, the past.[5]

In November 1881 he wrote to Baxter from Davos:

Your remarks about your business forcibly recalled the early
days of your connection, and the twopence that we once mus-
tered between us in the ever radiant Lothian Road.

O sweet Lothian Road . . .

O dear Lothian Road . . .[6]

A few weeks later he was writing in a similar vein:

Pray write to me something cheery. A little Edinburgh gossip,
in heaven's name. Ah! what would I not give to steal this
evening with you through the big, echoing college archway,
and away south under the street lamps, and to dear Brash's,
now defunct! [Brash was a Lothian Road publican who, according to Stevenson, sold gin in a peculiarly bad-tempered way.
He was the subject of some mocking verses by Stevenson.] But
the old time is dead also, never, never to revive. It was a sad
time too, but so gay and so hopeful, and we had such sport with
all our spirits and all our distresses, that it looks like a lamplit,
vicious fairy land behind me. O for ten Edinburgh minutes,
sixpence between us, and the ever glorious Lothian Road, or
dear mysterious Leith Walk! But here, a sheer hulk, lies poor
Tom Bowling – here in this strange place, whose very strange-
ness would have been heaven to him then – and aspires – yes,
C.B., with tears – after the past.

See what comes of being left alone. Do you remember
Brash? the L.J.R.? [the rebellious society founded by Stevenson, Baxter, Bob Stevenson, and others] the sheet of glass that
we followed along George Street? Granton? the night at Barry-
muirhead? the compass near the sign of the Twinkling Eye?
the night I lay on the pavement in misery?

I swear it by the eternal sky

Johnson – nor Thomson – ne'er shall die!

Yet I fancy they are dead too; dead like Brash.[7]

Johnson (or Johnstone) and Thomson were characters invented
by Stevenson and Baxter, roles they assumed in their correspondence when the mood took them. They were small-town hypocrites

who employed a racy Scots speech. In this curious exercise in role-taking Stevenson was in fact satirising in advance the kind of character who later in the century was to be treated with such sentimental affection in the literature of the Kailyard. Here is a letter from Johnstone (Stevenson) to Thomson (Baxter), one of a series, in which he reports how he was falsely accused of embezzling money from the church collection plate (*'No Bony-Feed wi' the plate'*) and as a result left the Church of Scotland and joined the sect of Morrisonians:

Thomson,

It's done. I'm a dissenter. I kenned fine frae the beginning hoo it would a' end; I saw there was nae justice for auld Johnstone. The last I tauld ye, they had begun a clash aboot the drink. O sic a disgrace! when, if onything, I rayther drink less nor mair since yon damned scandal aboot the blue ribbon. I took the scunner as faur back as that, Thomson; and O man, I wuss that I had just left the estayblishment that very day! But no, I was aye loyal like them that went afore me.

Weel, the ither day, up comes yoon red-heedit, pishion-faced creeter – him a minister! 'Mr. Johnstone,' says he, 'I think it my duty to tell 'ee that there's a most unpleisand fama about you.' 'Sir,' says I, 'they take a pleesure to persecute me. What is't noo?'

What was't? Man, Thomson, I think shame to write it: *No Bony-Feed wi' the plate*. Is'n that peetiful? The auld, auld story! The same weary, auld, havering claver 'at they tauld aboot Sandie Sporran – him that was subsekently hanged, ye'll mind. And wi' me – hoo improabable! But it a' comes o' that silly hash aboot my brither Sandy's trust: a thankless office, the trustees!

Whatever, I saw that I was by wi't. Says I, 'I'll leave the Kirk.' 'Weel,' says he, 'I think youre parfitly richt' and a wheen mair maist unjudeecial and unjudeecious observations. Noo, I'm a Morrisonian, an' I like it fine. We're a sma' body, but unco tosh. The prezentar's auld, tae; an' if ye'll meet in wi' our opeenions – some o' them damned hetrodox by my way o't, but a body cannae have a'thing – I mak nae mainner o' doobt but what ye micht succeed him. I'm a great light in the body; much sympathy was felt for me generally among the mair leeberal o' a' persuasions: a man at my time o' life and kent saw lang!

Aw. Johnstone   P.S. I'll hae to pay for the wean. In a so-ca'd Christian country! Mercy me![8]

The use of Scots, the playing of the part of Johnstone, were at the same time gestures of nostalgia for Scotland, ironic criticism of Scotland, and joyfully humorous literary play. Stevenson was more simply nostalgic in the verses ('my attempt at words to "Wandering Willie"') he sent to Baxter from Tautira in November 1888:

Home no more to me, whither shall I wander?
  Hunger my driver, I go where I must.
Cold blows the winter wind over hill and heather;
  Thick drives the rain, and my roof is in the dust.
Loved of wise men was the shade of my roof-tree,
  The true word of welcome was spoken in the door.
Dear days of old, with the faces in the firelight,
  Kind folks of old, you come again no more. . . .[9]

In February 1890 he wrote to Baxter from the steamer *Lübeck* between Apia and Sydney enclosing a poem that, he said, 'will say something to you'. Its title was 'To My Old Comrades' and it opened like this:

Do you remember – can we e'er forget –
How, in the coiled perplexities of youth,
In our wild climate, in our scowling town,
We gloomed and shivered, sorrowed, sobbed and feared?
The belching wind, the missile rain,
The rare and welcome silence of the snows,
The laggard morn, the haggard day, the night,
The grimy spell of the nocturnal town,
Do you remember? – ah, could one forget![10]

At this time, of course, he was in permanent exile. But even in earlier visits abroad he would indulge in nostalgic memories of Edinburgh, again a mixture of affectionate recall and harsh criticism. Writing to his parents from Royat in July 1884 he was reminded of Edinburgh by the bad weather and especially by the wind:

The imitation of Edinburgh is, at times, deceptive; there is a note among the chimney-pots that suggests Howe Street; though I think the shrillest spot in Christendom was not upon the Howe Street side, but in front, just under the Miss Graemes' big chimney-stack. It had a fine alto character – a sort of bleat that used to divide the marrow in my joints – say in the wee, slack hours. That music is now lost to us by rebuilding; another air that I remember, not regret, was the solo of the gas-burner in the little front room; a knockering, flighty, fleering, and yet spectral cackle. I mind it above all on winter afternoons, late, when the window was blue and spotted with rare raindrops, and, looking out, the cold evening was seen blue all over, with the lamps of Queen's and Frederick's Street dotting it with yellow, and flaring eastward in the squalls. Heavens, how unhappy I have been in such circumstances . . .[11]

He is remembering unhappiness with something very like affection.

None of these nostalgic passages, with their mixtures of longing and humour and criticism, quite prepares us for the great turning of his imagination to Scotland from Vailima, in spite of his keen interest in local politics and in the fictional potential of the South Seas (as shown notably in *The Ebb Tide* and *The Beach of Falesá*). Writing to Barrie from Vailima in November 1892 he mentioned that the three books he had just finished or had on the stocks were all on Scottish subjects – *David Balfour*, a novel called *The Young Chevalier* dealing with 'Prince Charlie about the year 1749' (which never got very far), and the novel centred on 'the immortal Braxfield', that he was to call *Weir of Hermiston*. Of course he had already published many other novels and stories set in Scotland, notably *Kidnapped, The Master of Ballantrae* and such shorter pieces as 'The Pavilion on the Links' and 'Thrawn Janet'. Even *Dr Jekyll and Mr Hyde*, though set in London, draws on Edinburgh for much of its topography, as Owen Dudley Edwards has demonstrated in a recent lecture. The reference to the Scottish novels is, however, less interesting than the observation that precedes it: 'It is a singular thing that I should live here in the South Seas under conditions so new and so striking, and yet my imagination so continually inhabit that cold old huddle of grey hills from which we come.'

David Balfour was published three months after the letter to Barrie. Its dedication, to Baxter, elaborates with almost desperate nostalgia the feeling expressed in that letter:

There should be left in our native city some seed of the elect; some long-legged, hot-headed youth must repeat to-day our dreams and wanderings of so many years ago; he will relish the pleasure, which should have been ours, to follow among named streets and numbered houses the country walks of David Balfour, to identify Dean, the Silvermills, and Broughton, and Hope Park and Pilrig, and poor old Lochend – if it still be standing, and the Figgate Whins – if there be any of them left; or to push (on a long holiday) as far afield as Gillane or the

Bass. . . .

You are still . . . in the venerable city which I must always think of as my home. And I have come so far; and the sights and thoughts of my youth pursue me; and I see like a vision the youth of my father, and of his father, and the whole stream of lives flowing down there, far in the north, with the sound of laughter and tears, to cast me out in the end, as by a sudden freshet, on these ultimate islands. And I admire and bow my head before the romance of destiny.

Stevenson expresses a similar mood in a letter to S.R. Crockett written from Vailima in May 1893: 'I shall never take that walk by the Fisher's Tryst and Glencorse. I shall never see Auld Reekie. I shall never set my foot upon the heather. Here I am until I die, and here will I be buried. The word is out and the doom written.' He goes on to talk of *Weir of Hermiston*, and an obvious association then leads to this:

Do you know where the road crosses the burn under Glencorse Church? Go there, and say a prayer for me: *moriturus salutat*. See that it's a sunny day; I would like it to be a Sunday, but that's not possible in the premises; and stand on the right-hand bank just where the road goes down into the water, and shut your eyes, and if I don't appear to you! well, it can't be helped, and will be extremely funny.[12]

The introduction of the funniness seems to be a deliberate piece of sturdy scepticism to ward off sentimentality and perhaps also to suggest that he is not as gullible in matters psychic as he might be thought to be.

Then there are the two well-known poems that sum up so much of Stevenson's feeling about Scotland towards the end of his life. One is the dedication to his wife of *Weir of Hermiston*:

I saw rain falling and the rainbow drawn
On Lammermuir. Hearkening I hear again
In my precipitous city beaten bells
Winnow the keen sea wind. And here afar
Intent on my own race and place I wrote. . . .

The other is the most moving of all Stevenson's poems of Scottish nostalgia, addressed to S.R. Crockett. Crockett had dedicated to Stevenson his book *The Stickit Minister* in these words: 'To Robert Louis Stevenson of Scotland and Samoa I dedicate these stories of that Gray Galloway land where About the Graves of the Martyrs The Whaups are crying – his heart remembers how.'

Stevenson was much moved by the dedication, as he wrote to

Colvin in August 1893: 'Did you see a man who wrote *The Stickit Minister*, and dedicated it to me, in words that brought tears to my eyes every time I looked at them. "Where about the graves of the martyrs the whaups are crying. *His* heart remembers how." Ah, my God, it does! Singular that I should fulfil the Scots destiny throughout, and live a voluntary exile and have my head filled with the blessed, beastly place all the time!'[13] In the same letter he told Colvin that Vailima was his home and his future tomb, 'though it's a wrench not to be planted in Scotland – that I never can deny – if I could only be buried in the hills, under the heather and a table tombstone like the martyrs, where the whaups and plovers are crying!' And so he wrote the poem:

> Blows the wind today, and the sun and the rain are flying,
> Blows the wind on the moors today and now,
> Where about the graves of the martyrs the whaups are crying,
> My heart remembers how!
>
> Grey recumbent tombs of the dead in desert places,
> Standing-stones on the vacant wine-red moor,
> Hills of sheep, and the howes of the silent vanished races,
> And winds, austere and pure.
>
> Be it granted to me to behold you again in dying,
> Hills of home! and to hear again the call;
> Hear about the graves of the martyrs the peewees crying,
> And hear no more at all.[14]

It is interesting that when Stevenson thought of death he thought of the Covenanters, those fiercely intolerant, self-righteous and persecuted men of God. As a child he had been fascinated by stories of their exploits and sufferings. His earliest book, proudly printed by his father when Stevenson was sixteen, was an account of an abortive rising by Covenanters in 1666, and, as he wrote to Barrie in December 1893, 'my style is from the Covenanting writers'. For all the cultivated bohemianism of his student days and later, for all his quarrel with his father on matters of religion, Stevenson remained always aware of his Covenanting heredity. 'When I was a child, and indeed until I was nearly a man, I consistently read Covenanting books', he wrote to Barrie in that same letter. 'Now that I am a greybeard – or would be, if I could raise the beard – I have returned, and for weeks back have read little else but Woodrow, Walker, Shields, etc.' A month before this letter he had written to Lord Rosebery about his attitude to the Lothians 'that beloved piece of country; beloved – and yet to me, in retrospect, almost hateful also'. He went on:

> I have been vigorously unhappy there in old days – more
> unhappy than in the death of all my friends, and a dose of
> leprosy, could make me now; my father is dead; many of my
> friends are 'lapped in lead'; and to return would be to me
> superlatively painful. Only I wish I could be buried there –
> among the hills, say, on the head of Allermuir – with a table
> tombstone like a Cameronian.[15]

The contradiction in his attitude to Scotland remained until the
end.

In the chapter entitled 'The Scot Abroad' in *The Silverado Squatters* Stevenson tried to come to terms with the special quality of a
Scotsman's feeling for his native country:

> A few pages back I wrote that a man belonged, in these days, to
> a variety of countries; but the old land is still the true love, the
> others are but pleasant infidelities. Scotland is indefinable; it
> has no unity except upon the map. Two languages, many
> dialects, innumerable forms of piety, and countless local pat-
> riotisms and prejudices, part us among ourselves more widely
> than the extreme east and west of that great continent of
> America. When I am at home, I feel a man from Glasgow to be
> something like a rival, a man from Barra to be more than half a
> foreigner. Yet let us meet in some far country, and, whether
> we hail from the braes of Manor or the braes of Mar, some
> ready-made affection joins us on the instant. It is not race.
> Look at us. One is Norse, one Celtic, and another Saxon. It is
> not community of tongue. We have it not among ourselves;
> and we have it, almost to perfection, with English, or Irish, or
> American. It is no tie of faith, for we detest each other's errors.
> And yet somewhere, deep down in the heart of each one of us,
> something yearns for the old land and the old kindly people.
>
> Of all mysteries of the human heart this is perhaps the most
> inscrutable. There is no special loveliness in that grey country,
> with its rainy, sea-beat archipelago; its fields of dark mount-
> ain; its unsightly places, black with coal; its treeless, sour,
> unfriendly-looking corn-lands; its quaint, grey castled city,
> where the bells clash of a Sunday, and the wind squalls, and
> the salt showers fly and beat. I do not even know if I desire to
> live there; but let me hear, in some far land, a kindred voice
> sing out, 'O why left I my hame?' and it seems at once as if no
> beauty under the kind heavens, and no society of the wise and
> good, can repay me for my absence from my country. And

though I think I would rather die elsewhere, yet in my heart of hearts I long to be buried among good Scots clods. I will say it fairly, it grows on me with every year: there are no stars so lovely as Edinburgh street-lamps. When I forget thee, Auld Reekie, may my right hand forget its cunning!

The happiest lot on earth is to be born a Scotsman. You must pay for it in many ways, as for all other advantages on earth. You have to learn the Paraphrases and the Shorter Catechism; you generally take to drink; your youth, as far as I can find out, is a time of louder war against society, of more outcry and tears and turmoil, than if you had been born, for instance, in England. But somehow life is warmer and closer; the hearth burns more redly; the lights of home shine softer on the rainy street; the very names, endeared in verse and music, cling nearer round our hearts. An Englishman may meet an Englishman to-morrow, upon Chimborazo, and neither of them cares; but when the Scots wine-grower told me of Mons Meg it was like magic. . . .[16]

It was not just Edinburgh and the Lothian hills that continued to haunt Stevenson's imagination. 'Thrawn Janet', set in a bleak Scottish landscape, 'the moorland parish of Balweary, in the vale of Dule', 'The Merry Men', 'a fantastic sonata about the sea and wrecks' as he described it to Henley, where he used his knowledge of off-shore islands (including his three weeks on Erraid when it was quarry and base for the building of the Dubh Artach Rock Lighthouse, also to be utilised in *Kidnapped*) acquired in his youthful tours to visit lighthouses, 'The Pavilion on the Links', where he invents episodes to suggest and symbolise the quality of the Scottish east coast near North Berwick, all show him exploiting Scottish topographical atmosphere. The sense of place, that served Stevenson so well as novelist and short-story writer, began with a sense of *Scottish* place. Before he ever began to think of *Kidnapped* he knew that the place where the kidnapping took place called for such a story. 'The old Hawes Inn at the Queen's Ferry makes a similar call upon my fancy. There it stands, apart from the town, beside the pier, in a climate of its own, half inland, half marine – in front, the ferry bubbling with the tide and the guardship swinging to her anchor; behind, the old garden with the trees. Americans seek it already for the sake of Lovel and Oldbuck, who dined there at the beginning of the *Antiquary*. But you need not tell me – that is not all; there is some story, unrecorded or not yet complete, which must express the meaning of that inn more fully.' So he wrote in

1882 in 'A Gossip on Romance': 'One thing in life calls for another; there is a fitness in events and places.' *Kidnapped* is as much a topographical as a historical novel. David Balfour's journeying from a Border village to Cramond and then to South Queensferry, his enforced voyage on the brig *Covenant* up the east coast of Scotland, through the stormy Pentland Firth, then south through the Western Isles until it is wrecked on a reef near Mull, his travels from Erraid to Mull, by ferry to Lochaline, on to Morven in Ard-gour, across Loch Linnhe to Lettermore; his discovery of Alan Breck between Lettermore (Leitir Mhor) and Ballachulish and their subsequent flight through the Pass of Corrieyairick, then south to Ben Alder, then across Loch Ericht and down its eastern shore to the head of Loch Rannoch, which they also cross before moving south to Balquhidder, the continued flight southward to the Allan Water to the Carse of Stirling and the Links of Forth and then the move eastward under the Ochils and by Alloa and Clack-mannan and Culross to the north shore of the Forth and then across it to South Queensferry – this is all realised in persuasively ren-dered detail, with the moods of the two characters correlated with the kind of country they pass through, and the state of the country-side reflecting the conditions and atmosphere prevalent in different parts of Scotland in the years immediately after Culloden.

Stevenson finished *Kidnapped* in Bournemouth in 1885, but he had begun thinking about the historical and other questions raised by the book at least as early as 1880, when we know from his letters he was involving himself in a serious study of Scottish, and espe-cially Highland, history. He writes to his parents from Davos in December 1880:

> It seems to me very much as if I were gingerly embarking on a *History of Modern Scotland*. Probably Tulloch will never carry it out. [John Tulloch, Principal of St Andrews University, who wrote on Scottish intellectual history and other topics but never in fact wrote a history of Scotland.] And, you see, once I have studied and written these two vols., *The Transformation of the Scottish Highlands* and *Scotland and the Union*, I shall have a good ground to go upon. . . .[17]

He never wrote these works on Scottish history. But the knowledge he acquired in his reading of the subject, illuminated by topo-graphy, enabled him to write *Kidnapped*. Most of the reading, thinking and imagining for the novel was done outside Scotland.

Stevenson's ambivalent attitude to Scotland was not merely the result of his ill health and the effect on his constitution of the

Scottish climate, though that provided a valid enough reason for
his seeking health in more congenial climes. He had in addition
what could be called a moral objection to the Scotland he knew
best, the Scotland, and especially the Edinburgh, of Victorian
gentility and respectability. His revolt against Victorian Edinburgh
is now well enough documented. What is perhaps not sufficiently
often noticed is that it was a *principled* revolt: Stevenson became a
bohemian on moral principle. The boy who delighted his mother
by playing at being a minister and acting out a church service, the
youngster who dictated a *History of Moses* to a proud parent, the
adolescent who wrote *The Pentland Rising* – and the father of his
flock at Vailima who invented and offered up his own prayers before
his assembled household, were all in many essentials the same
character. His Calvinist forebears were always in his blood, as he
very well knew. He was much concerned with morality and destiny.
His objection to the Christianity he saw preached and practised
around him in Victorian Edinburgh was a moral objection: he saw
it as hypocritical, as not adequately involved with true morality.
His cry 'Give me the publican and harlot' was not the cry of a
libertine but the cry of a man outraged at what passed for conventional pieties: indeed, it is hardly too much to say that in some
moods, in his student days, he saw himself almost as a Bohemian
Jesus putting compassion and understanding above the letter of the
law. This was not Calvinism, but it represented a moral preoccupation of a kind stimulated by the moral-religious arguments that
Calvinism had fostered in Scotland for generations. The bohemianism of Stevenson's student days, his passion for what he and his
friends called 'jink', designed to shock the respectable, his mem-
bership of the L.J.R., his adventures in Lothian Road, had, paradoxical though it may seem, a moral basis. The initials L.J.R.
appear to have stood for Liberty, Justice, Reverence. ('Yes, I remember the L.J.R., and the constitution, and my homily on Liberty, and yours on Reverence which was never written – so I never
knew what Reverence was.' Stevenson to Baxter, November 1891.)
Even if, as he ironically claimed, he never learned what reverence
was, the embodiment of the word in the title of the society of rebels
he helped to found is surely significant. Stevenson was never
simply a rebel against authority in order to free himself for unlimi-
ted self-indulgence. His deeply Scottish sense of morality troubled
him all his life.

This is not to say that Stevenson as an artist deemed it his duty to
preach morality. His various articles on fiction reveal no such

preoccupation. But in his mature fiction he was continually probing the conditions under which moral life can be recognised. Morality was never obvious, never the result of simply applying the rules. He was outraged that missionaries should have deliberately destroyed traditional beliefs and attitudes of native races in their attempt to convert them to Christianity. He wrote to Adelaide Boodle from Vailima in July 1894: 'Forget wholly and for ever all small pruderies, and remember that *you cannot change ancestral feelings of right and wrong without what is practically soul-murder*.' This is in a sense a very Scottish kind of *pietas*.

Morality was not easily recognisable. Long John Silver is in some ways the most admirable of the characters in *Treasure Island*, yet he is a villain. Jekyll and Hyde were the same person, just as Deacon Brodie the respectable Deacon of Wrights and Deacon Brodie the midnight burglar were the same person. In *The Master of Ballantrae* the problem is not simply that evil has style and *panache* while virtue is dull and uninteresting: it is that we cannot be altogether sure where the moral truth of the story lies and how far to trust the simple moral judgements of the narrator, Mackellar. In the great confrontation scene between Archie and his father in *Weir of Hermiston* Stevenson does a whole series of double-takes, shifting our sympathy from son to father and back again so that we have to ask ourselves (as Archie asks himself) whether our moral preconceptions which appeared at first to have marked Hermiston out as a morally repugnant character can be maintained in the face of the complex reality of experience. Indeed, the manipulation of moral sympathies that Stevenson achieves in this scene seems to me comparable, though on a different scale, to what Shakespeare achieves in swinging round the audience to sympathy with his hero in *Richard II*. Then there are the delicately ironic probings of moral double standards resulting from the white man's imposition of part of his culture on a primitive civilisation in *The Beach of Falesá*. Here again, and more obviously than in *The Master of Ballantrae*, we have a narrator who does not understand the moral implications of his own attitude or of the story he is telling, so that the story itself makes moral comments to the reader that are unavailable to the story-teller.

Thus does an inherited Scottish conscience work in a writer for whom Scotland provided, topographically, psychologically and socially, the 'objective correlative' for those moral problems and ambiguities that disturbed him all his life.

Stevenson was very much aware of the Scottishness of much of his writing. 'It's Scotch,' he remarked of *Kidnapped* in a letter to Baxter from Bournemouth in February 1886; 'no strong, for the sake o' they pork-puddens, but jist a kitchen o't, to leeven the wersh, sapless, fusionless, stotty, stytering South-Scotch they think saw muckle o'.' And again, writing to Baxter in December 1892 about *Weir*: 'It's pretty Scotch: the grand premier is taken from Braxfield (oh and by the bye send me Cockburn's *Memorials*) . . .'. In his very last letter to Baxter, written from Vailima in November 1894 less than a month before he died, he says: 'I say, should I not subscribe for the Scottish History Society? I am greatly taken with one I see referred to as being in the press: *The Forfeited Estates Papers*, 1745–6.'

Stevenson's awareness of being Scottish never faltered. When he was staying at Cuckfield Rectory in Suffolk in July 1873 he wrote to his mother:

> I cannot get over my astonishment – indeed, it increases every day – at the hopeless gulf that there is between England and Scotland, and English and the Scotch. Nothing is the same; and I feel as strange and outlandish here as I do in France or Germany.[18]

When he got back to Scotland he wrote to Mrs Sitwell of an encounter he had had with a labourer in Leven, Fife, who talked to him about education and politics, as only a Scot could have done. He contrasted his wit and wisdom with the dullness of the peasantry of Suffolk, and ended: 'You see what John Knox and his schools have done.'

Stevenson was to elaborate on this point in his essay 'The Foreigner at Home', written nine years later:

> But it is not alone in scenery and architecture that we count England foreign. The constitution of society, the very pillars of the empire, surprise and even pain us. The dull, neglected peasant, sunk in matter, insolent, gross and servile, makes a startling contrast with our own long-legged, long-headed, thoughtful, Bible-quoting ploughman. A week or two in such a place as Suffolk leave the Scotchman gasping. It seems incredible that within the boundaries of his own land a class should have been thus forgotten. . . . The first shock of English society is like a cold plunge. . . . A Scotch peasant will talk more liberally out of his own experience. He will not put you by with conventional counters and small jests; he will give you the best of himself, like one interested in life and man's chief end.[19]

In December 1892 Stevenson wrote to Barrie from Vailima: 'I am proud to think you are a Scotchman . . . There are two of us now that the Shirra might have patted on the head.' This is to claim fellowship with Barrie as a fellow Scot: it is also to bring the two of them into fellowship with a third Scot, greater than either – 'the Shirra', that is, Sir Walter Scott. Stevenson did not often associate himself as a writer with Scott, though he refers to him with admiration a few times in his letters. 'That is what I always envied and admired in Scott; with all that immensity of work and study, his mind kept flexible, glancing to all points of natural interest.' He once wrote to his father that *Guy Mannering*, *Rob Roy* and *The Antiquary* are 'all worth three *Waverleys*', which is perhaps an odd judgement but at least shows an involvement with Scott's novels, which we know he had read avidly. Nevertheless, he was not the same kind of Scottish writer that Scott was. Scott was a genuine historical novelist, for whom historical change and the movement out of an outworn social code to a new one provided a context in which to examine the relation between character and history. For Stevenson, history was a setting for the presentation of modern problems. Scott would never have written that scene in *Kidnapped,* at the end of the quarrel between David and Alan, where David wallows in eloquent self-pity: this is brilliantly done, but it is Stevenson speaking, not a character in history. The difference in character between David and Alan, which Stevenson saw as the difference between Lowlander and Highlander, was to him more interesting psychologically and morally than historically. So when Stevenson involved Barrie as jointly associated with him in the Scott tradition, he was not thinking of the kind of writer each was – otherwise how could he possibly have involved Barrie? – but of the fact that here were three *Scottish* writers who had made it or were on the point of making it. There was another trilogy of Scottish writers of whom he was proud to be one, as we shall see.

For all the emotion with which Stevenson read S.R. Crockett's dedication to him of *The Stickit Minister* and for all the autobiographical confessionalism of his letter to Crockett in May 1893, which was quoted earlier, he never sought any kind of identification with Crockett as a writer and, in the few letters he wrote him, kept a certain distance. Indeed, in his very first letter to Crockett, from Saranac Lake in the Spring of 1888, he professed that he could not make out his signature:

DEAR MINISTER OF THE FREE KIRK AT PENICUIK, – For O, man, I canna read your name! – That I have been so long in

answering your delightful letter sits on my conscience. . . . I
get a good few such; how few that please me at all, you would
be surprised to learn – or have a singularly just idea of the
dulness of our race; how few that please me as yours did, I can
tell you in one word – *None*. I am no great kirkgoer, for many
reasons – and the sermon's one of them, and the first prayer
another, but the chief and effectual reason is the stuffiness. I
am no great kirkgoer, says I, but when I read yon letter of
yours, I thought I would like to sit under ye. And then I saw ye
were to send me a bit buik, an says I, I'll wait for the bit buik,
and then I'll mebbe can read the man's name, and anyway I can
kill twa birds wi' ae stane. And, man! the buik was ne'er heard
tell o'.'[20]

The drop into Scots signifies not only a fellow feeling for another
Scot; it has a slightly mocking effect, as though he regards Crockett
as a faintly comic character in a Scottish story. And the P.S. is
sternly critical:

Don't put 'N.B.' in your paper: put *Scotland*, and be done with
it. Alas, that I should be thus stabbed in the home of my
friends! The name of my native land is not *North Britain*
whatever may be the name of yours.[21]

Is there a suggestion here that Crockett's Scottishness is aimed at
the edification of an English audience? Perhaps not, for Stevenson
had not yet read any of Crockett's work and never passed an opinion
on the Kailyard. But he was clearly irritated by 'N.B.', as many
other Scots were to be later.

In his last letter to Crockett, that of May 1893, he addresses him
formally as 'Dear Mr Crockett' and begins by protesting: 'I do not
owe you two letters, nor yet nearly one, sir!' He ends with a
paragraph of somewhat patronising advice (Crockett was ten years
younger than Stevenson and *The Stickit Minister* was his first work
of fiction):

I am sure you chose wisely to keep your country charge. There
a minister can be something, not in a town. In a town, the most
of them are empty houses – and public speakers. Why should
you suppose your book will be slated because you have no
friends? A new writer, if he is any good, will be acclaimed
generally with more noise than he deserves. But by this time
you will know for certain.[22]

Stevenson's use of Scots was sometimes nostalgic (as frequently
in his letters to Baxter), sometimes humorous, sometimes ironi-
cal, and sometimes a sign of deep personal emotion. In the dia-

logue of his Scottish novels it was none of these things: it was an
attempt to provide psychological, social and historical appropriate-
ness. In the confrontation between Archie and his father in *Weir of
Hermiston*, the father's mocking Scots and the son's clipped and
defensive English illuminate splendidly the situation that is being
presented. In *Kidnapped* and *The Master of Ballantrae*, Scots is
used in dialogue less dramatically but no less appropriately. He
wrote to his French translator, Marcel Schwob, that in both these
novels he 'should be prepared for Scotticisms used deliberately'.
Stevenson's poems in Scots, often in 'Standard Habbie' or the
Burns stanza, are often in a faded post-Burns tradition but sometimes they reflect a genuine, often nostalgic, emotion that finds it
necessary to express itself in a language associated with his native
country. 'Ille Terrarum' is such a poem. Here are its concluding
stanzas:

But noo the auld city, street by street,
An' winter fu' o' snaw an' sleet,
Awhile shut in my gangrel feet
    An goavin' mettle;
Noo is the soopit ingle sweet,
    An' liltin' kettle.

An' noo the winter winds complain;
Cauld lies the glaur in ilka lane;
On draigled hizzie, tautit wean
    An' drucken lads,
In the mirk nicht, the winter rain
    Dribbles an' blads.

Whan bugles frae the Castle rock,
An' beaten drums wi' dowie shock,
Wauken, at cauld-rife sax o'clock,
    My chitterin' frame,
I mind me on the kintry cock,
    The kintry hame.

I mind me on yon bonny beild;
An' Fancy traivels far afield
To gaither a' that gairdens yield
    O' sun an' Simmer:
To hearten up a dowie chield,
    Fancy's the limmer![23]

Nostalgia is not the most productive of literary emotions, and it has been the curse of much Scottish literature. But Stevenson had more right to be nostalgic than most. His nostalgic Scots poems are agreeable, sometimes and in some ways moving, but they operate in a faded mode. In 'A Lowden Sabbath Morn' he can forget all his early criticisms of the religion in which he was brought up and evoke with affection – sometimes amused affection – the human details of a country church service. Some of his Scots poems are comic or at least facetious ('The Blast – 1875', 'Their Laureate to an Academy Class Dinner Club', 'The Scotsman's Return from Abroad'). Once, in 'The Spaewife', he achieves a poem in Scots that strikes a note both proverbial and popular: it is interesting that in this, probably the best known of all Stevenson's poems, he avoids the over-used Burns stanza in favour of a lilting four-line stanza with six stresses in each line and the lines rhyming in pairs. It has no suggestion of autobiography or nostalgia, but sounds a note of popular wisdom.

It was with the Scottish poets that Stevenson most identified himself. He felt a very special kind of kinship with Robert Fergusson, the Edinburgh poet who died in the public Bedlam of the city in 1774 at the age of 24. (He was born exactly a hundred years before Stevenson.) In May 1894 Stevenson wrote to Baxter from Vailima:

I have now something heavy on my mind. I had always a great sense of kinship with poor Robert Fergusson – so clever a boy, so wild, of such a mixed strain, so unfortunate, born in the same town with me, and, as I always felt rather by express intimation than from evidence, so like myself. Now the injustice with which the one Robert is rewarded and the other left out in the cold sits heavy on me, and I wish you could think of some way in which I could do honour to my unfortunate namesake. Do you think it would look like affectation to dedicate the whole edition [the projected Collected Edition of Stevenson] to his memory? The sentiment which would dictate it to me is too abstruse; and besides I think my wife is the proper person to receive the dedication of my life's work. At the same time – it is very odd, it really looks like transmigration of souls – I feel that I must do something for Fergusson; Burns had been before me with 'The Gravestone'. It occurs to me that you might take a walk down the Canongate and see what condition the stone is in. [Fergusson's gravestone, erected by Robert Burns when he was in Edinburgh in 1787, in the Canongate churchyard.] If it be at all uncared for, we might repair it and perhaps add a few words of inscription. . . .

Suppose we do what I have proposed about Fergusson's monument. I wonder if an inscription like this would look arrogant:

This stone, originally erected by Robert Burns, has been repaired at the charges of Robert Louis Stevenson and is by him re-dedicated to the Memory of Robert Fergusson as the gift of one Edinburgh lad to another.

In spacing this inscription I would detach the names of Fergusson and Burns but leave mine in the text; or would that look like sham modesty and is it better to bring out the three Roberts?[24]

Writing in April 1891 to W. Craibe Angus, who was organising a Burns exhibition in Glasgow, Stevenson testified to his 'perennial' interest in Burns, and added:

When your hand is in, will you remember our poor Edinburgh Robin? Burns alone has been just to his promise; follow Burns, he knew best, he knew whence he drew fire – from the poor, white-faced, drunken, vicious boy that raved himself to death in the Edinburgh madhouse. Surely there is more to be gleaned about Fergusson, and surely it is high time the task was set about. I may tell you (because your poet is not dead) something of how I feel: we are three Robins who have touched the Scots lyre this last century. Well, the one is the world's, he did it, he came off, he is for ever; but I and the other –! what bonds we have – born in the same city; both sickly; both pestered, one nearly to madness, one to the mad-house, with a damnatory creed; both seeing the stars and the dawn, and wearing shoe-leather on the same ancient stones, under the same pends, down the same closes, where our common ancestors clashed in their armour, rusty or bright. . . . You will never know, nor will any man, how deep this feeling is: I believe Fergusson lives in me.[25]

We know now that it was a gross exaggeration to think of Fergusson as a 'white-faced, drunken, vicious boy', just as we know that Stevenson exaggerated Burns's personal moral faults or at least failed to understand the strains under which he lived. But it is interesting that it was partly this sense of a common debauchery that linked him to Burns and more especially to Fergusson. I have said that Stevenson was a Bohemian on moral principle, not out of wanton vice or debauchery. Yet here we see him identifying him-self with a poet whom he considered to be simply vicious. Some-thing about the combination of personal moral inadequacy and

poetic genius appealed strongly to Stevenson, strongly enough
indeed for him to think of himself as one of a trilogy of Scots poets
when his genius was for prose and he had little more than a talent
for verse. Because Burns made it, and lived somewhat longer, he
does not get the strong compassion afforded to Fergusson. And
then of course there was the common Edinburgh element. However we interpret all this, Stevenson's view of the 'three Robins',
expressed more than once, shows a special kind of commitment to
a significant Scottish poetic tradition and at the same time illumi-
nates that compulsion to probe moral ambivalence that runs right
through Stevenson's work and which can be associated with his
Scottish Calvinist background. (Moral ambivalence may at first
sight appear to be remote from Calvinism, but, as Hogg showed in
his *Memoirs of a Justified Sinner,* it is precisely the Calvinist
doctrine of predestined election, regardless of good works, that can
lead to the most appalling moral ambivalence of all – a man who
feels himself to be one of the elect indulging in vice because he
knows that it cannot affect his election. Burns saw this in 'Holy
Willie's Prayer'. Stevenson used this insight somewhat differently.)

Stevenson was within a few months of his death when he wrote
to Baxter about repairing Fergusson's tombstone and associating
himself with Fergusson and Burns in the inscription. (This was
never done.) In the same letter he copied out the dedicatory poem
to *Weir of Hermiston,* with its deeply nostalgic feeling for the hills
south of Edinburgh and for the city itself. Fergusson's grave in the
Canongate kirkyard and the graves of the martyrs on the 'hills of
home' were both haunting his imagination in his last days. It was a
symbolic combination: Bohemianism and Calvinism, Art and Morality, the City and the Country. We might add, Samoa and Scotland, but that is a different kind of counterpointing: all the other
pairs of opposites (if they were opposites) were included in Scotland as Stevenson saw her.

References
1 *The Letters of Robert Louis Stevenson,* selected and
   edited by Sidney Colvin [*Letters*] (New York 189)
   vol. I, 156-7.
2 *RLS:Stevenson's Letters to Charles Baxter,* ed.
   DeLancey Ferguson and Marshall Waingrow [*Baxter*]
   (New Haven 1956) 337.
3 *Edinburgh: Picturesque Notes,* Collected Works,
   Skerryvore Edition (London 1925) vol. XXVI, 3.
4 *Collected Poems,* ed. Janet Adam Smith (London 1971)
   376.

5   *Baxter*, 48.
6   ibid., 95.
7   ibid., 98.
8   ibid., 126.
9   ibid., 239.
10 ibid., 256.
11 *Letters*, I, 376-7.
12 *Letters*, II, 344.
13 Quoted in *Collected Poems*, 518.
14 ibid., 283-4.
15 ibid., 518.
16 *From Scotland to Silverado*, ed. James D. Hart
    (Cambridge, Mass. 1966) 210-11.
17 *Letters*, I, 225.
18 *Letters*, I, 53.
19 *Memories and Portraits*, Collected Works, Skerryvore
    Edition (London 1925) vol. XXI, 8-9.
20 *Letters*, I, 118.
21 ibid., 119.
22 ibid., II, 344.
23 *Collected Poems*, 148-9.
24 *Baxter*, 354-5.
25 *Letters*, II, 266-7.

MICHAEL BALFOUR

The First Biography

In Peacock's novel *Headlong Hall*, there is a passage where a landscape architect Mr Gall (said to be modelled on Capability Brown) is describing the principles he works on: 'I distinguish the picturesque and the beautiful and I add to them, in the laying-out of grounds, a third and distinct character which I call unexpectedness.' 'Pray Sir', asks another member of the party, Mr Milestone, 'by what name do you distinguish this character when a person walks round the grounds for the second time?'[1]

Twenty years ago I published in the T.L.S. a couple of articles describing how my father came to be the official biographer of his second-cousin Louis. I based my work in part on papers then in my possession but now in the National Library of Scotland. I have worked over these papers and other materials again but I have no fresh material – or indeed fresh conclusions – to offer.

First however I should perhaps correct the title of this essay. In a letter to E. L. Burlinghame of Scribners on 6 August 1899 Lloyd Osbourne said reproachfully that 'three unauthorised lives' had already appeared.[2] Study of the Bodleian Library Catalogue leads me to think that this statement was better justified than many of Lloyd's remarks. Would it then be profane to suggest that my father's book, published in 1901, might be called 'The Authorised Version'?

Before I describe its genesis however I would ask you to bear with me while I explain how the Balfours get into this act at all. To do so properly, I must go back twelve generations, to the year 1500, when there were various families of my name living in adjacent parishes in Fife. There is still a Balfour Castle on the banks of the Orr shortly before it flows into the Leven and the most plausible etymological derivation of the name is 'Place on the Orr'. Unfortunately records prior to 1500 are scarce and it is impossible to

establish a connection between these other families and my earliest
known ancestor. He was Alexander, to whom in 1502 King James
IV granted the tack of Inchrye, near Newburgh. Persons called
Alexander Balfour crop up twelve times in the Scots Exchequer
Rolls between 1480 and 1508 and there is nothing to show how
many of them are identical, except that in 1480 there is mention of
senior and junior. But the one who settled at Inchrye is almost
certainly the man who between 1499 and 1508 is mentioned five
times as holding the responsible offices of *cellararius* and *butel-*
larius to the king. By 1518 Alexander of Inchrye had been dead for
some years and it is tempting to suppose he was killed at Flodden
but there is no evidence whatever for this. He was succeeded by
David who at an unknown date and for an unknown reason moved
from Inchrye to Powis in Logie Parish, northeast of Stirling. When
in *Kidnapped* Louis made his David Balfour cross the Forth at the
old bridge of Stirling, he was making him pass through the very
Parish in which the real David Balfour who was presumably his
ancestor had actually lived, only, as my father mentioned in a
footnote, the writer had no idea that the name David had occurred
in the family! Today the other interest for us of this David Balfour
is that he died on 11 July 1580.

His fourth son James was in 1589 appointed a Minister at St Giles'
in Edinburgh and seventeen years later was a member of the Scots
delegation to the abortive Hampton Court Conference, along with
his cousins Andrew and James Melville. James' grandson was a
Clerk of Session and *his* son a merchant who played a leading part in
launching the Darien Company. After its failure, he died of disap-
pointment and his son, another James, was advised to disown the
debts which were his principal inheritance. He refused to do so,
with the result that when after the Act of Union the English
government provided the shareholders with compensation, he ob-
tained his portion. He used it in 1718 to buy a house built in 1638 by
one Gilbert Kirkwood on a Peel ridge in the country between
Edinburgh and Leith.

Between 1718 and 1893 there were five successive Balfour Lairds
of Pilrig, though the last added Melville to the name. The second
was appointed in 1754 Professor of Moral Philosophy at the University of Edinburgh. I have no reason to think he was a particularly
bad philosopher but I am afraid he certainly was not as good a
philosopher as the rival candidate who however was regarded by
the appointing committee of Ministers with, to be fair, no little
justification, as being 'unsound on the fundamentals'. I imagine I

need not mention that candidate's name. It was the Professor, described as a cousin, whom David Balfour is made to visit in the third chapter of *Catriona*.

The Professor's son and third Laird – a commission agent and corn merchant – had five children. The third, Lewis, became Minister of Colinton and was R.L.S.'s grandfather. The second, John, took over the corn business and lived in Pilrig Street; he was my great-grandfather. His second son by his first wife qualified as a doctor in Edinburgh and then joined the Medical Service of the British Army, in which, having worked with Florence Nightingale to reform it and having laid the foundations of its statistics, he became a Surgeon-General. His only son, my father, was born and educated in England. On leaving Oxford, he qualified as a barrister but never practised and instead did a succession of odd jobs, which included bear-leading Bertrand Russell's elder brother round North America. By 1891 his parents were dead. He was interested in Japanese art and had a fancy to see its native land. His private income was modest but travel costs in those days were low. I have Cook's bill for the first-class journey from London to Yokohama – £130. Having got so far, it seemed natural to suggest a visit to the second-cousin in Samoa although their only previous meeting (and that Louis failed to remember) had been in a party to a London pantomime. Here is the reply to his approach: 'We are very glad to have your visit. No errands from Honolulu'.[3] He cannot for a moment have supposed as he crossed the Pacific that the trip would lead nine years later to his becoming his host's biographer.

Louis had originally intended Henley to perform that function but had begun to change his mind as early as 1885 while he was still in Bournemouth. He accordingly added a codicil to his will, naming his wife instead as his first choice. He asked her however, if she felt able to comply, to allow Henley to give his own account 'of matters that he knows best' – in other words, the 'years of Jink and Brash' in Edinburgh. Correspondingly he begged Henley, if Fanny should 'desist from her present profession of willingness to execute the task', to carry along with him in it the counsels of Fanny and Colvin.[4] In view of the tensions which were already beginning to develop between the three, I think it can fairly be said that 'the mind boggles' at anticipating the number of rows to which any attempt to carry out this request must have led.

Fanny resented Henley's boisterous visits on the ground that they over-excited Louis and left her to cope with a reaction after they were over. In March 1888 Henley retaliated with an accusation

that Fanny had plagiarised and made money out of a story which
had first occurred to Katherine de Mattos, sister to Louis' cousin
Bob. Louis was always a sensitive man and particularly where his
wife was concerned. The ensuing row, well documented in the
R.L.S.–Baxter correspondence, was of monumental dimensions
and clearly put paid for good and all to any idea of Henley being the
person primarily responsible for delineating the friend of his youth.

Accordingly in December 1888 Louis proposed in a letter which
Lloyd Osbourne his step-son was to open after his death, that
Colvin should produce a modest biography, but only as part of a
collection of 'reliquiae, little verses, and certain of my letters'.[5] The
main object was to provide money for Louis' family to live on. But
the codicil contained what was to prove a well-judged caution:
'You must beg Colvin not to run away with all the profits by
incessant alteration and delay. That is the danger of S.C. But for my
sake and my family's, he will make an effort to conquer this beset-
ting sin'.

A variant of the same proposal was revived in a letter of January
1893 to Charles Baxter, though by then it had got complicated by
the decision that, for reasons which were unstated but which
Baxter was said to know well, not all the correspondence could be
allowed to pass through Colvin's hands.[6] I can only surmise that it
contained uncomplimentary references to Colvin himself – or possibly he did not want Colvin to know all the details of the row with
Henley. Because of this, the correspondence was to be collected by
Baxter and a selection made from it by my father before it was
turned over to Colvin. 'In this way, I believe we ought to be able to
parry any unpleasantness.' Louis however went on 'to protest
wholly against the idea of a biography, the circumstances of my
pleasing career render this impossible. At the same time a certain
introduction (say by Colvin) might be suitable.'[7] Fanny at that time
wanted the correspondence published forthwith, so that Louis
himself could do the selection, but he and Baxter ruled out the idea
as impracticable.

After Louis' death the sealed letter to Lloyd was opened and
acted on. The papers from Vailima, including manuscripts, were
brought back to London by my father and Baxter, who also collected the correspondence which was gone through by my father
before being given to Colvin. The latter began with the relatively
easy task of publishing the regular letters which Louis had written
to him from Samoa between 1890 and 1894; these came out in the
autumn of 1895 as 'Vailima Letters'. They were considerably expur-

gated. The letters to other correspondents proved more numerous
than was expected; arranging the publication of *Weir of Hermiston*
and other fragments also took time, so that work went ahead
slowly. Only too naturally the introductory sketch, more and more
spoken of as a full-scale biography, got put on one side. In the
summer of 1898 Fanny, growing restive, came with Lloyd to London with the object of hastening things on. According to Lloyd's
son, he and Fanny had never wanted Colvin to be the biographer,
presumably because of his lack of sympathy for the whole South Sea
existence. They hoped that the tactful if devious way of taking it out
of his hands would be to let him by delaying provide them with a
good excuse.[8]

Colvin must have shown reluctance to pin himself down, for
Fanny explained in a letter to him that 'to find the one last object of
my life shifting like a mirage before my eyes is almost more than I
can bear. I want something definite. Cannot you give me that?'[9]
The question of turning the job over to someone else must also
have been mentioned, for on 25 June Colvin wrote to Lloyd: 'I
quite understand, and do not resent, the mistrust of my powers of
finishing the work which previous delays have produced in your
mother's mind and yours. If I lose what has been the great hope of
my heart, through the unavoidable conditions of my life and health,
it will be a great blow to me indeed but one which I shall try to bear
without bitterness.'[10] In the end it was agreed that two volumes of
letters and one volume of biography should be published in the
autumn of the following year and that, if Colvin was unable to
finish a full 'Life' of 120,000 words, he would, rather than let the
date slip, compress it into a briefer form. With that rather shaky
reassurance Fanny and Lloyd went off to winter in Madeira, after
she had undergone a serious operation for gall-stones.

Colvin did in fact manage to draft three chapters during the
winter. But his duties at the British Museum that winter included
the compiling of a catalogue raisonné for an exhibition of Rem-
brandt. He never mentioned this to the Stevensons, who, when
they heard of it, thought it was another book undertaken of his own
free will and were correspondingly incensed. The double effort
proved too much for him and on 31 March 1899 he wrote to Fanny,
still in Madeira, that 'my head has quite broken down again and I
cannot go on with the biography for the present'.[11] He described his
state of health at some length and suggested that the two volumes
of letters should come out in the following autumn as planned,
with notes and an introduction but without a proper biography.

Lloyd – not Fanny – replied that 'such being the unfortunate state of affairs, let me say in all frankness that you must give up the task. We have waited – I think you will admit how patiently and generously – for more than four years; we can wait no longer. You must allow us to make new arrangements.'[12] To Baxter he wrote that 'it is positively and absolutely understood that Colvin's connection with the Life is at an end'.[13] Colvin in a reply which Lloyd described to Baxter as 'sad and smooth' appeared to accept the decision,[14] describing it as 'the failure of what had been the great hope and interest of my life'.[15] To start with, he got the idea that the letters were to be taken away as well, but this would seem to have been a real misunderstanding and was soon removed, possibly with help from Baxter who wrote early in May a letter to Fanny which has not survived but which he described as 'an onslaught – she deserves it'.[16] But Colvin also suspected Lloyd of wanting to write the biography himself. I cannot swear that such an idea was never conceived but I much doubt if it was ever treated seriously. Colvin had proposed to Baxter that men of letters and friends of Louis should be asked for their views on it, with the implication that these would be highly unfavourable. He explained his own position as being that, if the biography were left in his hands, he would do it some day and do it, as he honestly believed, better than anyone else could. But the date, given the state of his health and the prior claims of his official duties, must remain *quite indefinite*. If under these circumstances the family should find a properly equipped and sympathetically inclined man of letters willing to undertake it, Colvin would have no quarrel and would not dream of playing dog-in-the-manger. He must have spoken in these terms to Fanny and Lloyd on their return, for in Mid-May he wrote to Baxter that 'it has been an inexpressible relief to find myself on the old affectionate terms with the family'.[17] At the same time I suspect he had a sneaking hope that a suitable man of letters would prove hard to find.

It looks however very much as though Fanny and Lloyd already had their eyes, not on anyone whom Colvin would regard as a man of letters but on my father. Within a week of reaching London, Fanny wrote to him saying she was most anxious to see him in connection with the Life: 'It is plain that Colvin is not fit any more to do the work so we have definitely taken it from him.' They met on 4 June when she pressed him to take over.[18] His qualifications were not at first sight altogether convincing. His only published work was a description of the British educational system. He had only known Louis for the last two years of the latter's life and then only intermittently. Some doubts on this score would seem to have been expressed by Colvin's friend Mrs Sitwell in what Fanny described as 'a sea-urchin of a letter written by a pig-face'.[19]

In reply Fanny argued that the very fact of not being a professional man of letters was an advantage; the choice could not be construed as a slur on Colvin. Secondly my father had known Louis more intimately than almost anyone else in the world just at the time when he was at the zenith of his powers. I would like to enlarge a little on this. In the South Seas Louis not only matured to become, as Mr Furnas has so well explained, almost a different person, someone too who wanted more in companionship than Fanny could give. The arrival of his forties, a time of life when most people are apt to revise for the better their opinion of the previous generation, found him sundered by 'continents and continental oceans' from the city of his parents and the haunts of his youth. With improved health, the exile's thoughts turned increasingly to his native land. In my father's words, 'the love of country which is in all Scots and beyond all others lies deepest in the Celtic heart flowed back on him again and again with a wave of uncontrollable emotion'. But Fanny and Lloyd were Americans who had only known Scotland as visitors – somewhat critical visitors under a critical gaze. My father may never have lived in Scotland but he knew and loved it and was a member of the family. He was into the bargain well-acquainted with British and European literature and art – one of his great-uncles was a William Buchanan who in 1804 wrote a book called *Memorials of Painting* and travelled all over Europe hunting for paintings, primarily for the Angerstein collection which formed the nucleus of the National Gallery – Titian's *Bacchus and Ariadne* being the best known. He had even been round many of the islands which Louis had visited in the *Equator* and *Janet Nichol*, so that he was uniquely equipped to deal with the South Sea period. And he had one further qualification on which Colvin could not possibly have reckoned. He was keenly alive to the structure of English prose, as I know well from his comments on my own youthful efforts. I am not saying that the prose of the biography is an immortal masterpiece but I do suggest that it has the essential merit of clarity and does not intrude between reader and subject.

My father could see as clearly as anyone the objections to his doing the job and for some time hesitated to accept it. But the months in Vailima had been the great experience of his life. The bond which they constituted with Fanny was strengthened by his having inherited, along with devotion to her husband, that husband's valuation of her. He never ceased to insist that, but for her care, Louis would have died long before 1894. Without being blind to her defects, and even less blind to those of Lloyd Osbourne, he would never allow them to distract attention from her merits or tolerate the criticism in which many encountering her superficially were apt to indulge. He therefore decided that her request was an obligation which must be fulfilled.

His name would seem to have been first mentioned to Colvin in mid-July. In the interval there had been a flaming row between Colvin and Lloyd over the question of the payment to be received by the former now that he was merely to edit the letters. Today I find it hard to avoid surprise that there could have been so much fuss over a mere £83! Colvin wanted to take less immediately and then share in any later profits, an arrangement from which with a book destined to go into so many editions he would undoubtedly have benefited. Lloyd however insisted on a settlement once and for all. Colvin behaved with greater dignity throughout and in the end gave way. But before that happened, strong things were said on both sides, chiefly to Baxter who, as so often, acted as conciliator. An exacerbating factor was that Louis and his heirs had paid out some £800 in premiums on a life insurance policy for Colvin, and felt that this generosity was inadequately appreciated.

At the end of July Lloyd followed up his mother's informal intimation by formally asking Colvin to agree to the nomination of my father, saying that 'although in your April letter you resigned the task absolutely into our hands, I felt then and have always felt that yours must be the principal voice in choosing another biographer'[20] – a way of putting things which makes it strange that he never asked Colvin for suggestions but instead asked his assent to a suggestion of their own – though one must in fairness add that they offered to seek an alternative if Colvin so desired. But Lloyd also asked that whoever was chosen should be assured by Colvin that he entirely relinquished the task himself.

The use of the word 'entirely' sparked off another row. Colvin took up what was by no means an unjustifiable position. If the family insisted that a biography must be written forthwith, he would on all accounts welcome my father as the man to do it. Moreover he would give all reasonable help, though he would not be disposed to hand over what he described as 'my personal material which is considerable and the result of many years of love and labour'. On the other hand he was not prepared to renounce definitely doing his own book at some future date. 'Having regard to the fact that no one could possibly write the inner and mental history of RLS with the same knowledge that I can, I am not prepared to renounce my life's purpose in the matter for good and all.'[21]

He went on, however, to question whether a biography was needed urgently and quoted 'literary figures in London' as thinking that it wasn't. Even if this were true, it was unwise, since he knew how keen Fanny was to get a biography published quickly and had often been told by her that his delay had already caused a loss of money. His stance produced firm letters from Lloyd demanding that he hand over all the Stevenson papers in his possession and guarantee my father a clear field for the next four years.[22] Colvin is said to have taken legal advice as to his rights over the papers but in the end, after he and Lloyd had met, did hand over 'an accumulation of RLS papers which had gathered under his charge' as well as those brought to him from Samoa. I do not think these included all his letters from Louis or those which Louis had written to Mrs Sitwell in 1873–6. Copyright in these would legally have belonged to the recipients.

Colvin also wrote on 13 August to my father as follows:

Please let me make things quite plain as between you and me about this RLS business. I don't pretend to think that the family are acting wisely in taking the Life out of my hands; certainly they are going dead against the strong feeling of all L's literary friends in London: but of that they refuse to inform themselves.

But if there is to be a substitute for me, there is no-one, as I told them with perfect sincerity, whom I should so much welcome as yourself. Only this is not to be understood as meaning that I forego my right and purpose of telling the story of RLS my own way at some future time. Yours, if you finally decide to undertake it, will be the official Life: mine must be its own book. I daresay we could quite well understand each other so as not to make them clash much even in matter: certainly I have not the slightest intention of making mine clash with yours in date. I shall keep mine till yours has had a two-year chance, very likely longer. I could not say this to Lloyd, because he has an unlucky way of putting things, in writing at least, that puts my back up and makes concession impossible: but I can say it quite freely to you. The next thing is to stop chatter. There will be lots of tiresome gossip and some uproar, unless we seem to be acting together. What I propose to do therefore is to suppress my private feelings in the matter altogether, and to say in the Preface to the forth-coming book of letters that 'want of health and leisure has prevented my finishing the biographical part, which has consequently been undertaken by L's cousin, my friend Mr Graham Balfour'.[23]

To this my father drafted the following reply (which to the best of my knowledge went off without alteration):

As far as I am concerned, I am quite content with your proposals viz to give my book a two years start and to announce in your Preface in the terms which you suggest.

I do not think that there is any reason why the two books should clash. Of the years which you know best, I know but little, and your critical work is quite beyond my grasp. Out of the pass in which we find ourselves, I think we can quite well come with harmony and honour, and that I am sure is what will best serve Louis' memory and our love for him.[24]

And so it was left. In the end, Colvin waited not two years but twenty-two before he published anything and then it was only a chapter in his reminiscences.

Though one may have considerable sympathy for him, he *was* all along trying to have his cake and eat it. He wanted to set the line for posterity's view of Louis, yet would neither get on with doing so or even commit himself to a date. Was want of health and leisure the whole explanation? In the end, only want of leisure was mentioned in the introduction to the Letters and no explanation at all was offered by E. V. Lucas in *The Colvins and their Friends*. I cannot help suspecting other reasons, though I am not suggesting that Colvin made them explicit – even to himself.

The first lies in his relation with Mrs Sitwell, whom he would have married long before but for the fact that she had a husband and he a mother who had to be supported, and whom he did marry when both were free in 1903. But it was she to whom Louis had poured out his soul in his twenties and with whom he might well have sought a closer relationship had she not gently but firmly rebuffed him. (Incidentally, I understand her to be the original of Mrs Barton Trafford in Somerset Maugham's *Cakes and Ale*.) To describe this episode fairly would not have been easy for Colvin, knowing all that he did. I am not however inclined today to attach as much importance to this obstacle as I did twenty years ago.

Colvin need not have said much more in a biography than appeared in those letters from Louis to the lady, which he had already published. Only those of his acquaintance who knew more might have thought him a trifle ingenuous, as might posterity.

I increasingly believe that the real lion in the path was the prospect of a long series of battles with Fanny and Lloyd as to what went in and what did not. There were two spheres where argument was likely. The first concerned what was said about the South Seas. Colvin, as we have seen, assumed that 'no one could possibly write the inner and mental history of RLS with the same knowledge that I can' – in spite of the fact that for the last third of the years they were acquainted, the years of Louis' fullest maturity, Colvin's knowledge derived solely from correspondence and that he had shown scant sympathy for the idea of living permanently in the South Seas. He was unlikely to play up the period to the extent Fanny would wish.

The other sphere, Louis' youth, lent itself even more to argument. There had already been clashes over what was or was not to be included in the Letters and he had written to Lloyd 'I am afraid it is not possible, with any regard for eventual truth, to avoid upsetting the idyllic fictions about Louis' Edinburgh days . . . derived from Aunt Maggie whose peculiar gift of disguising all facts at all unpleasant whether from others or herself, you must have known by your own experience'.[25] Aunt Maggie had died in 1897 but Fanny was likely to rival her in anxiety to sweep youthful escapades under the carpet. But any toning down of the picture to appease the family was likely to make all the more inevitable an outburst from Henley who believed the Louis he had known and loved to have been stolen away from him by Fanny and who must be expected to take his revenge – as indeed he did though, as Mr Furnas brilliantly detected, what cut deepest was not any act of Fanny's but the revelation of a stab-in-the-back by Louis himself.

Among the papers brought home by my father from Samoa had been a letter from Henley to Louis, probably written in 1881: 'If you have a chance of reading Colvin's biography of you, you will see him veiling (in print) his blushing cheek and passing over certain of your earlier years in a manly annd sorrowful silence.'[26] To which Louis replied that 'Chapter 2 "Youth in Edinburgh" is likely to be a masterpiece of the genteel evasion'. It may indeed have been realisation of the difficulty of doing anything other than evade which led Louis in 1893 to say that 'the circumstances of my pleasing career render a biography impossible'. And in his 1885

codicil he had said that 'It is never worth while to inflict pain even
upon a snail for any literary purpose' and that 'I would rather be
misunderstood than cause any pang to anyone I have known, far
less loved'. Pangs unfortunately can be caused by silence as well as
by statement.

I reckon that my father's book runs to 150,000 words, 25 per cent
longer than the 120,000 contemplated by Colvin, who later said
that, if there was need for anything in the short run, it was for a
popular Life which would not be too large or too dear. Approxi-
mately three-eighths of it deals with the South Seas and Samoa,
where Louis spent six-and-a-half of his forty-four years. The only
indelicate fact which my father knowingly suppresssed was Louis
and Fanny's anticipation of the parson at Grez. When a story to this
effect was brought to his notice four months before his book came
out, he replied that he did not think it was the affair of himself or
the public. Today we would probably say that it *is* the affair of the
public because it throws light on the character of the two people
involved. Even so, I don't see that it tells us much about them we
shouldn't have guessed anyhow. And nothing was said to disguise
it, while the shortness of the interval between Fanny's divorce and
the subsequent marriage was clearly stated despite some pressure
for employing the carpet-sweeper. The pages devoted to youth in
Edinburgh are suggestive rather than specific – whether that
amounts to evasion is not for me to say. Colvin thought that the
bohemian aspects of life in Edinburgh and Barbizon had been
shirked.[27] But after the way in which we now know him to have
expurgated the Letters, he was not in much of a position to make
such a criticism. He also considered that too few unpublished
writings had been included, forgetting that, in objecting to the job
being taken out of his hands, he had advanced as one of his reasons
the fear that an inexperienced author might print writings un-
worthy of R.L.S., 'youthful things he would have burnt if he were
here'.[28]

The drawback about leaving things unpublished but unburnt is
that before long the human itch for knowledge and novelty will
tempt somebody into printing them. The drawback about leaving
people to read between the lines is that they will read not too little
but too much. Yet where would literary historians be for employment if they did not occupy themselves in setting the balance right?
In the 1920s Colvin and my father chose to hold their peace because
they were confident that this would happen. Today I feel they have
been justified.

I have gone on long enough. But before I end, let me quote from a couple of letters. The first is from Henry James – not the superbly characteristic letter he wrote after reading my father's book which you will find in full in my 1960 T.L.S. article, but one he wrote in November 1901 after reading Henley's 'Pall Mallic' against the book. I am not aware that it has ever been published.

> Your two good letters have cheered me under the disgust of the *Pall Mall Magazine* – which I but tardily acquired . . . I speak of the disgust of Henley's lugubrious effort but I am not sure that it excites in me that positive emotion or any emotion so kin to interest. For, surely, it is poor, poor, poor, & really of a hole-and-corner quality of taste, feeling and form. I had read Henley but little but I supposed him a more 'important' pen. The interest the thing *does* present is of a documentary sort in respect to H himself – and in that particular is curious: the long-accumulated jealousy, rancour – I suppose of invidious vanity, so getting the better of a man of his age and experience that, your book at last making the cup overflow, he tumbles it all about before a mocking world. Only indeed that world isn't mocking, but stupid, passive, easily muddled – which ensures him a certain impunity.[29]

The other is a letter of New Year's Day 1919 from my mother to my father, who was then in France.

> I went this day to —'s wedding party where were many fine folk both small and great. And before that, I called upon the Colvins. And, my Dear, the whirligig of Time has never failed us yet. SC went over, as between old and dear friends, the whole episode of the Life being given to you! It began by his saying 'Tell Graham I've just been reading his book again and finding it very, *very* good.' He then said, 'I was nasty and jealous about it for a long time, because it was given to him in order to anger me'. 'Well,' said I, 'never was man more taken aback, or, at the first moment, less ready to undertake it, than Graham.' 'I know that,' said he, 'He was very nice about it all through. And of course he knew Samoa, and he *was* the right person for that. But what I am now struck with, is that he has done the earlier part so well: the part he didn't know about personally'. So there, I came away like a dog with two tails, trying to wag both at once.[30]

References

1   Thomas Love Peacock, *Headlong Hall,* chapter 4.
2   Lloyd Osbourne to E. L. Burlinghame, 6 August 1899,
    Beinecke Collection, Yale University.
3   Stevenson to Graham Balfour, June 1892.
    In the author's possession.
4   Will, 10 October 1885, National Library of Scotland.
5   Stevenson to Lloyd Osbourne, December 1888,
    National Library of Scotland.
6   Stevenson to Charles Baxter, in *RLS : Stevenson's
    Letters to Charles Baxter,* ed. DeLancey Ferguson and
    Marshall Waingrow (New Haven 1956) 322.
7   ibid.
8   Alan Osbourne, *Times Literary Supplement,*
    25 March 1960.
9   Fanny Stevenson to Sidney Colvin, 26 June 1898,
    Beinecke Collection.
10 Sidney Colvin to Lloyd Osbourne, 25 June 1898,
    Beinecke Collection.
11 Colvin to Fanny Stevenson, 31 March 1899, Beinecke
    Collection.
12 Lloyd Osbourne to Colvin, 14 April 1899, Beinecke
    Collection.
13 Lloyd Osbourne to Baxter, 17 April 1899, Beinecke
    Collection.
14 Lloyd Osbourne to Baxter, 28 April 1899, Beinecke
    Collection.
15 Colvin to Lloyd Osbourne, 22 April 1899, Beinecke
    Collection.
16 Baxter to Colvin, 4 May 1899, Beinecke Collection.
17 Colvin to Baxter, 17 May 1899, Beinecke Collection.
18 Graham Balfour to R. Balfour, 4 June 1899, National
    Library of Scotland, see also Fanny Stevenson to
    Colvin, National Library of Scotland.
19 Fanny Stevenson to Graham Balfour, November 1899,
    National Library of Scotland.
20 Lloyd Osbourne to Colvin, 30 July 1899, Beinecke
    Collection.
21 Colvin to Lloyd Osbourne, 1 August 1899, Beinecke
    Collection.
22 Lloyd Osbourne to Colvin, 4 and 10 August 1899,
    Beinecke Collection.
23 Colvin to Graham Balfour, 13 August 1899, National
    Library of Scotland.
24 Balfour to Colvin, National Library of Scotland.
25 Colvin to Lloyd Osbourne, 13 July 1899, Beinecke
    Collection.
26 Stevenson to Henley and Henley to Stevenson, 1881,
    National Library of Scotland.
27 Colvin to Graham Balfour, 1901, National Library of
    Scotland.

28 op. cit., note 27.
29 Henry James to Balfour, November 1901, National
    Library of Scotland.
30 Rhoda to Graham Balfour, 1 January 1919, National
    Library of Scotland.

TREVOR ROYLE

The Literary Background to
Stevenson's Edinburgh

In the *Scotsman* of 8 and 9 November 1889, in two rambling articles
which assess Edinburgh's literary history, David Masson, Professor of Rhetoric and English at the University of Edinburgh, noted
with some alarm that the *Edinburgh Directory* for that year had
listed only sixty-two publishers within the city and that of those
mentioned, the majority were concerned with the publication of
educational and religious works. He continued in similar vein to
complain that, 'one can recollect the time when there were more
newspapers in Edinburgh than there are now', and that apart from
the continued existence of *Blackwood's Magazine* and *Chambers'
Journal*, Edinburgh had lost its crown as a publishing centre.[1]

By the end of the century, that other famous Edinburgh publication the *Edinburgh Review* was a Scottish magazine by name only
and had long since moved to London. It had started life in 18
Buccleuch Place in October 1802, the inspiration of three advocates
with Whig inclinations: Henry Brougham, Francis Horner and
Francis Jeffrey, and an Anglican chaplain with a sharp wit, Sydney
Smith. Its publisher was Archibald Constable who had been described by Scott as the 'prince of booksellers', and a man of whom
Lord Cockburn had said, 'the literature of Scotland has been more
indebted than to any other of his vocation'.[2]

One of those founders, Sydney Smith, had said that 'it requires a
surgical operation to get a joke well into a Scotsman's understanding',[3] but there was nothing funny about the *Edinburgh Review*.
Its first issue of 750 copies quickly sold out and it soon created an
almost insatiable demand. By 1807 the circulation was 7,000 and it
reached its peak eleven years later with monthly sales of well over
14,000 copies. Francis Jeffrey became the permanent editor in 1803
and he vested the role of editor with a previously unheard of dignity
and professionalism. He was paid a salary of £300 a year by Con-

stable, who also took the astounding step of arranging for substantial sums to be paid to the magazine's contributors. Jeffrey was a fluent, quick-witted man who managed to combine an active legal and political career with his work on the *Review*. He went on to become a Member of Parliament and Lord Advocate, but it was the editor who encouraged young writers like Thomas Carlyle, who enjoyed the greatest renown in literary circles still prepared to forgive him for telling Wordsworth that *The Excursion* would never do. 'Our dialogue was altogether human and succesful; lasted for perhaps twenty minutes (for I could not consume a great man's time), turned upon the usual topics, what I was doing, what I had published – German Romance Translations, my last thing; "We must give you a lift!" an offer which in some complimentary way, I managed, to his satisfaction, to decline' – is the somewhat stark style of Carlyle's first meeting with Jeffrey in his offices in George Street.[4]

Another formidable contributor to the *Edinburgh Review* had been Sir Walter Scott, but a savage thirty-five page review by Jeffrey of *Marmion* in April 1808 ended Scott's patience with the magazine's political and literary stance and he turned instead to writing for John Murray's Tory *Quarterly Review*, which was published in London, and later to championing a new magazine which had been established to challenge the Whig dominance of the *Edinburgh Review*. By the time of Masson's article, *Blackwood's Magazine* had sunk into a torpor, and was publishing obscure, learned articles; tales of travel and adventure which reflected the country's growing interest in its Empire; it had developed a haughty, hidebound conservatism in politics and an editorial stance that was very far removed from the stormy days of its foundation in October 1817.

Blackwood's Magazine had been the brainchild of William Blackwood, an Edinburgh bookseller who had been one of the first of his trade to move out of the cluttered confines of the traditional bookselling quarter of Parliament Square and the South Bridge and had set up shop in the Georgian New Town, at 17 Princes Street. It quickly became a centre of literary taste, 'the only great lounging bookshop in the New Town of Edinburgh . . . an elegant oval saloon, lighted from the roof, where various groups of loungers and literary dilettanti are engaged in looking at, or criticising amongst themselves, the publications just arrived by that day's coach from town' – is the loving description of the saloon from that treasure-trove of nineteenth-century literary gossip, John Gibson Lockhart's *Peter's Letters to His Kinsfolk*.[5]

It was from that office that Blackwood published his first magazine under the editorship of two minor writers James Cleghorn and
Thomas Pringle but its quaint mixture of odd scientific facts and
other nonsenses masquerading as literature was not guaranteed to
cause a faster heartbeat in literary circles. Something more nimble
was required and so Blackwood turned to three men to revitalise
the magazine's flagging fortunes: John Wilson, or 'Christopher
North' as he is more popularly known, John Gibson Lockhart and
James Hogg. Blackwood was not disappointed by them. When the
citizens of Edinburgh awoke on the morning of 21 October 1817
they found not only a new magazine on sale but a publication
whose centrepiece was the translation of, 'a Chaldee MS which is
preserved in the great library of Paris . . .'.[6] What followed in the
'manuscript' was a satire written by the three new editors, couched
in the language of the Old Testament, of the leading literary and
political personalities of the day. It was a tour-de-force and, for a
few brief days, *Blackwood's Magazine* stood at the centre of the
British literary stage. Half the city roared with laughter at its now
obscure and half-forgotten references (Scott appears as 'the great
magician who dwelleth in the old fastness which is by the River
Jordan')[7] and the other half bellowed with rage.

Lockhart and Wilson, though, were pests as editors and lashed
out at their fellow writers under the guise of anonymity and then
trembled in fear that they be detected. Included in that first issue
were slashing attacks on Keats and the 'Cockney School of Poetry',
on Coleridge's *Biographia Literaria* and a derisive article on Leigh
Hunt. The outrage caused by the appearance of the magazine only
enhanced its popularity, and as often happens, the threat of lawsuits
only served to increase the demand for further satirical attacks. Mrs
Grant of Laggan wrote in her memoirs that the city was 'in an
uproar about *Blackwood's Magazine* which contains in a very irre-
verent and unjustifiable form, a good deal of wit and cunning
satire'.[8] James Hogg, rightly cautious about the *literati*'s attitude to
him returned to his farm in Ettrick where he wrote to Scott pleading
with him, 'For the love of God, open not your mouth about the
Chaldee MS'.[9] Even Lockhart and Wilson, while continuing to
exhort Blackwood to 'keep your mind in good fighting condition'
were forced by the outrage of their enemies to flee the city for
refuge in Windermere.[10]

By and by the storm caused by that early issue died down and
although the magazine continued to publish its hoaxes, rib-
poking and learned tomfoolery, much of the criticism was pub-

lished for its own sake, and within a few years *Blackwood's* was a spent force. Stevenson was never published in its pages, an article on Raeburn was turned down in the Spring of 1876 and for the rest of his life he maintained a healthy distrust of the magazine, especially of its arbiter of literary taste, Margaret Oliphant, who had succeeded Christopher North. Like him she was a fierce critic of the innovatory in letters. 'Mrs Oliphant seems in a staggering state', wrote Stevenson from Samoa in December 1889, 'from *The Wrong Box* to *The Master* I scarce recognise either my critic or myself.'[11]

Towards the end of his life Stevenson relented in his attitude, but William Blackwood III, the fourth Blackwood to control the magazine's destiny, was in no mood to bargain with Charles Baxter who was acting as agent. The letters between Stevenson and Baxter are worth quoting *in extenso* because they say much about the impending problems which were facing publishers who were unable to compete with their London counterparts in terms of financial security, distribution and promotion of their authors. Stevenson had, simply, priced himself out of the market for a smallish Edinburgh publisher.

> Vailima, 1 December 1892
>
> . . . Apropos – I have a novel on the stocks to be called *The Justice Clerk* (Weir of Hermiston). It is pretty Scotch: the grand Premier is taken from Braxfield (Oh, bye the bye send me Cockburn's *Memorials*), and some of the story is – well – queer. The heroine is seduced by one man and finally disappears with the other man who shoots him. Now, all this, above all after our experience with *Falesá*, don't look much like serial publication; if the worst comes to the worst we shall of course do without that. But it has occurred to me that there is one quarter in which the very Scotchness of the thing would be found a recommendation and where the queerness might possibly be stomached. I mean Blackwood. And I think it might be worthwhile to sound the Blackwood's on the subject. I had sworn a great oath that they should never have anything of mine, but there is no sense in cutting off your nose to spite your face . . .[12]

In his reply Baxter did not mince his words about the canny publisher's attitude.

> Edinburgh, 20 January 1893
>
> I've seen Bill Blackwood, who is staggered at what I've asked him: £2,000 for the serial rights. You see, an old humdrum

house has no machinery for selling these all over the world.
But here is the sort of idea he ettles at: to pay £2,000 for the
Magazine rights *and* an edition of say 3 or 5,000. I say, not good
enough, and I'll see what better can be done. Besides, Bill
Blackwood's money comes in slow, and not sure.[13]

It was not that William Blackwood was without literary taste: he
published, amongst others, Oscar Wilde, Stephen Crane and Joseph Conrad, and although, as we shall see, he had a blind spot
concerning detective fiction, he was considered to be one of the
better literary publishers of his time.

However, through their foresight, those pioneers of the book
trade had discovered a new reading public and it had a voracious
appetite. Constable had been the first to recognise that money was
to be made out of the market, and to meet the new demands other
publishers set themselves up in the city, amongst them being
William and Robert Chambers who had started as booksellers in
Leith Walk and had then moved to Hanover Street before setting up
as publishers in Thistle Street where they remain to this day. They
published *Chambers' Journal* and an Encyclopaedia and although
the magazine is long since defunct, Chambers remains at the forefront of British reference book publishing. Both the brothers, who
were born in Peebles, made substantial contributions to their adopted city. William was Lord Provost in 1865 and 1868 and was a great
benefactor of the Church of St Giles, while Robert's work as a writer
includes that formidable wealth of information, *The Traditions of
Edinburgh* which was written in 1823 at a time when its author
wanted to capture some of the grandeur of an age that was rapidly
passing from human memory.

In 1827 at 57 South Bridge, Adam Black had purchased the copyright of the *Encyclopaedia Britannica,* and like many others of his
day, slowly transformed himself from bookselling to publishing.
He built up a list that specialised in philosophy, science and theo-
logy and, as the firm expanded, he brought in his nephew Charles
as a partner in 1834. By then he had moved his office to 27 North
Bridge, a building that once housed the General Post Office. It was
to be his penultimate Edinburgh address; there was a brief stay at 6
North Bridge before the firm moved to London in 1889. On the
other side of the city the firm of Thomas Nelson moved from their
Grassmarket offices to Hope Park near the Meadows to set up their
revolutionary rotary printing press. They pioneered the production
of cheap classics for the mass market, and when fire destroyed their
works, they moved, undeterred, to larger premises in Dalkeith

Road, beneath the Salisbury Crags.

The other great Victorian publisher was the long-established house of Oliver and Boyd which had been founded in 1778 by Thomas Oliver as a printing press in the High Street near the Netherbow. He had been joined by George Boyd in 1807 and in 1820 they had moved to their picturesque and warren-like offices in Tweeddale Court to push themselves to the forefront of Scottish educational publishing. On a momentous day in 1836 a young bookseller's apprentice called James Thin, employed by James Macintosh of 5 North College Street, called at Oliver and Boyd and was impressed with what he saw, '. . . they had gradually developed into publishers, printers and bookbinders, and were the only firm who at that time carried on these departments'.[14] James Thin founded his own bookselling business opposite the university on South Bridge in 1841, and eventually became the largest bookseller in the city, but that early visit was remembered sixty years later when his sons became controlling directors of Oliver and Boyd together with John Grant, the other large Edinburgh bookselling business.

Although publishing might not have been the force it once was, in Stevenson's Edinburgh days, there was sufficient evidence that Scotland's capital was still a bookish city. The Public Library Act of 1850, sponsored by a Scotsman William Ewart, member of parliament for Dumfries, had been adopted in Scotland in 1853 although it was not until 1886 that the first public library was started in the city. Later, in 1895, with funds from Andrew Carnegie, it opened in its present splendid headquarters on George IV Bridge. The Advocates' Library which had been founded on the initiative of Sir George Mackenzie of Rosehaugh in the seventeenth century was still housed in a piecemeal fashion in the city and it was not until 1925 that it became the National Library of Scotland. The library housed the nation's finest collection of books and manuscripts and early supporters for its elevation to national status were Thomas Carlyle in 1874 and David Masson who was able to claim that, 'next to London, and perhaps to Oxford, Edinburgh has the largest provision of books in any city in the British Empire'.[15] There was a good selection of booksellers in the city and another bright star on the cultural horizon was the formal opening of the Royal Lyceum Theatre in Grindlay Street on 10 October 1883 with a gala performance starring Ellen Terry and Henry Irving. At the other end of the scale, for those who had ears to hear, were the ridiculous poetry readings given by William McGonagall, poet and tragedian, who had been born in the city in 1825, the son of a handloom weaver.

Although he spent most of his life in Dundee, he was a frequent visitor to Edinburgh and his poem in her praise would have been considered a doubtful joke had it not come from the hand of McGonagall, a man whom his contemporary the editor William Power described, aptly, as 'the Ossian of the ineffably absurd'.[16]

At the time of the Lyceum's opening, a young medical graduate of the University of Edinburgh sent *Blackwood's Magazine* a story, 'The Actor's Duel' which was hurriedly turned down by the editor, William Blackwood III. Several other attempts were made, with other stories, until the young doctor tired of banging his head against the magazine's stolid management had sent his work to the newly founded *Strand Magazine*. The July 1891 issue of that magazine made Dr Arthur Conan Doyle famous overnight with the publication of *A Scandal in Bohemia*, the first of the Sherlock Holmes' stories.

Conan Doyle had been born in Edinburgh on 22 May 1859 in his parents house at 11 Picardy Place. After a rigid education at Stonyhurst, a Catholic boarding school, he studied medicine at Edinburgh in the class of Dr Joseph Bell, a pioneer in forensic medicine who was to become one of the models for Sherlock Holmes. Like his near contemporary Stevenson, Conan Doyle disliked Edinburgh for its grim winter and equally bleak university which he described as a mother 'of a very stoic and Spartan cast who conceals her maternal affection with remarkable success'.[17] He could see no future for himself in Edinburgh and as soon as he had graduated he left his tiny cluttered flat in Howe Street and set up practice in Southsea, a suburb of Portsmouth. Apart from the accident of birth, Edinburgh can make little claim on Conan Doyle. The city does not figure as a backdrop in his writing, but his studies under distinguished doctors like Bell, Maclagen and Rutherford, and his knowledge of the insanitary horrors of the Old Town gave him fuel enough for his detective fiction, together with a glimpse perhaps of the living proof of Calvin's dynamic aspect of evil which lies at the roots of *Dr Jekyll and Mr Hyde*. The thought of living in Edinburgh never crossed his mind. Success lay elsewhere and like many other Scots of his generation he took the road south, to enormous success, to a knighthood in 1902 and to a rich and fulfilled life.

Conan Doyle, though, was in good company at the University of Edinburgh in the decade that followed Stevenson's partial attendance at the classes 'through the big echoing college archway'. Amongst them was Samuel Rutherford Crockett, whose novel *The Stickit Minister*, which was dedicated to Stevenson, was so successful that it enabled him to give up his calling as a Free Church minister in 1893 and turn to full-time writing. Crockett had known the pangs of hunger while a student, and in later, more successful days he claimed that he had existed on oatmeal, penny rolls and milk. It was not uncommon for undergraduates to be poverty-stricken – there were no grants, and bursaries were fiercely competed for – and many students looked for part-time employment to ease the burden of their lives. Mostly, these were fairly menial tasks, but one student had determined from an early age that he would be a writer, and so he made a name for himself through the pleasant and remunerative occupation of writing theatre criticism and book reviews for the *Edinburgh Courant*. His name was James Matthew Barrie.

Crockett and Barrie became leading members of the school of writing that is now known as the Kailyard, which presented a sloppy picture of a never-never land of rural virtue presided over by the discerning eye of the local minister. Helping to manipulate that rash of sentimentality was Sir William Robertson Nicoll, the editor of the *British Weekly* who was also a patron from his London office of the other two main Kailyarders, 'Ian Maclaren' – John Watson, a Church of Scotland minister – and Annie S. Swan.

Born near the village of Coldingham in Berwickshire in 1859, Annie S. Swan spent her early years in Edinburgh, in a house which stood at the top of Easter Road, 'then a lovely country lane bordered by fields and hedges, white with May bloom, and pink wild roses in summer'.[18] Later her father farmed at Gorebridge in Midlothian and he sent his daughter to be educated at the Queen Street Ladies College in Edinburgh, soon to become the Mary Erskine School. She started writing early, winning a Christmas story competition in the *People's Journal* while she was at school and achieving overnight success with her second novel *Aldersyde*. By then she was married to a medical student and living in a flat in Morningside where she kept open house for her student friends. At that time, too, Margaret Oliphant became the first of many critics to attack the bitter-sweet sentimentality of her novels, but Annie S. Swan was unabashed, claiming in her autobiography, that 'the public had no fault to find with it and asked for more. After all, it is the reading public which passes the final judgement on any book'.[19] Despite that rap over the knuckles, Annie S. Swan was an assiduous collector of friends and during her stay in Edinburgh, and later in Musselburgh she was the unlikely companion of Patrick Geddes and his wife Anna, pioneers of modern social work and town planning who were responsible for much restoration work in the Lawnmarket and for the construction of Ramsay Garden on the site of Allan Ramsay's 'Goose Pie' house on Castle Hill.

Later Annie S. Swan took up residence in London, the home of her erstwhle critic Margaret Oliphant. Born in April 1828 in Wallyford near Musselburgh, Margaret Oliphant married her cousin, an impoverished artist, and quickly discovered that hack writing was a reasonable means of financial independence. She lived for a time in the eighteen-sixties in Fettes Row and from her pen flowed a succession of biographies, novels, histories and over two hundred articles and reviews for *Blackwood's Magazine*. Today most of Mrs Oliphant's work is forgotten – we remember Stevenson's work and not her views of it. She wrote too much too quickly and with too little intellectual equipment to do her work justice, but she did succeed in keeping her family's head above water.

Connected with her in the Blackwood group was William Edmonstoune Aytoun who was married to the youngest daughter of Christopher North. Almost as prolific as Margaret Oliphant, Aytoun wrote a series of humorous stories for the magazine, including 'How we got up the Glenmutchkin Railway', a droll exposé of railway mania which indicted both unscrupulous speculators and gullible buyers; and 'How I stood for the Dreepdailly Burghs', a satire on political sycophancy which reads as well today as if it had been written last week. A lawyer to trade, Aytoun became Professor of Rhetoric and Belles-Lettres in Edinburgh in 1845, but during his own lifetime he was perhaps best known for *The Bon Gaultier Ballads* which he wrote with Sir Theodore Martin, and for his *Lays of the Scottish Cavaliers*, a series of ballad romances from the annals of Scottish history.

Aytoun was also the severest critic of the so-called Spasmodic School of poets whose number included P. J. Bailey, Sydney Dobell and Alexander Smith. In their work, the poet-hero leads a life of mysterious spiritual insularity which forces him to commit bizarre acts in striving to discover the secrets of the universe. In May 1854 Aytoun published a review of an imaginary Spasmodic poem, *Firmilian, or the Student of Badajoz* which became such a *cause célèbre* that he followed it up by actually writing the poem and publishing it three months later. The publication of *Firmilian* – it tells the story of a student who is engaged on a history of Cain and who, in order to equip himself for the task, embarks on a series of crimes with absurd results – effectively destroyed the popularity of the Spasmodic poets.

Among their number was Alexander Smith who was at that time employed in the registry of the university. Despite their literary differences, he and Aytoun became friends eventually and Smith went on to write one of the best early travel books, *A Summer in Skye,* which contains a stunning description of Edinburgh in winter. There had been a long tradition in the city of writing private literature and this was continued during the nineteenth century. Edward Bannerman Ramsay, the episcopalian Dean of Edinburgh wrote the immensely successful *Reminiscences of Scottish Life and Character* which went through twenty editions after its original publication. Another professional man and occasional writer was Dr John Brown – 'the Scottish Charles Lamb', as he was known – whose collection of essays, *Rab and His Friends,* is a miniature masterpiece, at its best in his understanding of the human nature of many dogs. As the century wore on, Brown's medical practice became of less importance to him and he devoted more time to encouraging a delight in wit and the art of conversation, accomplishments which won him the friendship of many leading men of his day.

Thackeray visited Brown in 1863 and like other literary visitors was impressed by the city's scenic grandeur. The best known, and certainly the most popular, visitor was Charles Dickens, who had first come to Edinburgh in 1834 as a young journalist on the London *Morning Chronicle* to cover the granting of the freedom of the city to Earl Grey, the hero of the Reform Bill. As there was no building large enough to accommodate the two thousand guests, a marquee had been constructed in the grounds of the High School and it was lit by a huge gas chandelier borrowed from the Theatre Royal. It should have been a glittering occasion, but, as Dickens reported, some of the guests could not contain their appetites and fell upon their dinner before the arrival of the guest of honour, Earl Grey, 'and this is, perhaps, one of the few instances on record of a dinner having been virtually concluded before it began'.[20] Dickens returned to the city on a happier errand in 1841 to accept its freedom, and he was welcomed back in 1858 when he read his *Christmas Carol* to a large, enthusiastic audience in the Music Hall.

Charlotte Brontë arrived in Edinburgh on a brief visit in 1850 and praised 'the Scottish national character . . . which gives the land its true charm, its true greatness'.[21] And in 1854, Harriet Beecher Stowe found Edinburgh 'full of spirits of those who, no longer living, have woven a part of the thread of our existence'.[22] Today, when we contemplate the gaunt fortress of the St James' Centre which dominates the eastern skyline of the city, we would also do well to remember John Ruskin's warning to the citizens of Edinburgh, made in a lecture given in the Philosophical Institution on November 1853. 'Before you boast of your city, before you venture to call it yours, ought you not scrupulously to weigh the exact share you have had in adding to it or adorning it, to calculate seriously the influence upon its aspect which the work of your own hands has exercised?'[23] Sadly, it is a warning that has all too often gone unheeded in recent years.

There were of course many other writers connected with the city in mid century. Kenneth Grahame, the future author of *The Wind in the Willows* was born at 30 North Castle Street, opposite Sir Walter Scott's old house, on 3 March 1859 but he left the city in infancy and was brought up in England. Thomas Carlyle had left the city in 1828, disappointed by the failure of his application for an academic post. He returned in 1866 to become the university's Lord Rector but, saddened by his wife's death, the visit brought him recognition but little happiness. In a fit of melancholy, Hugh Miller, a master of polished prose, the author of *The Old Red Sandstone*, took his life in his house in Portobello on 2 December 1856. Charles Kirkpatrick Sharpe, a link with the days of Sir Walter Scott, was still a familiar, if bizarre figure in Princes Street – 'an old gentleman, very peculiarly attired in a faded surtout of utterly antique fashion' as David Masson described him;[24] and David Macbeth Moir, author of that pawky Scottish novel *Mansie Wauch*, was a much-loved and revered figure.

That tartan-clad slough of Balmorality, the Kailyard, claimed many a Scottish writer and as the century progressed literature in Scotland became more parochial and inward-looking. It was indicative of the changing times that David Masson should round off his literary survey of Edinburgh with the death in 1854 of Christopher North – 'the long-known, long-admired and still magnificent Christopher North'.[25] And yet Wilson was much to blame for a good deal of the ossification that had gripped literary Edinburgh in Masson's lifetime. An intellectual snob, he adopted a crude, hectoring tone to match his distrust of imaginative literature and turned instead to the sloppy and to the sentimental. He was a menace as an editor and arbiter of taste – a double-dealer to friend and foe – and he represents all that was bad in the literature of the period. An examination of his relationships with James Hogg and John Galt hardly bears out Masson's confident description of the man as Edinburgh remembered him shortly after his death.

Wilson was, like Sharpe, a link with the Edinburgh of Sir Walter Scott when the city was still a literary centre of note, a time which a contemporary witness, Robert Forsyth, has described as 'polite and intelligent',[26] and a society which Lord Cockburn characterised in his *Memorials* as never having been 'better, or indeed so good, since I knew it, as it was about this time'.[27] Cockburn went on to remark that the city had lost its intellectual glitter by 1820 and he mourned the passing of the age, fearing a future which would only bring 'little literature, and a comfortless intensity of political zeal'.[28] By mid century, as we have seen, his first prediction had come true.

Cockburn, in a sense, lived two lives. One was that of the polite Charlotte Square lawyer with an honourable position in the city's society and the other was that of 'Cocky', the country gentleman with a house at Bonaly in Colinton and a penchant for plodding the Pentland Hills. He regretted the passing of the old Scotland and yet he was motivated by the need for social change; like others of his age he was Scottish, but half-anglicised, orphaned (to use Karl Miller's memorable description) both from his Scottish past and his British future, a paradox not uncommon in early nineteenth-century Edinburgh and one to which Stevenson himself was to turn.

'On with the new coat and into the new life! Down with the Deacon and up with the robber!' cries Deacon Brodie in the play which Stevenson wrote with W. E. Henley.[29] Dr Henry Jekyll draws 'steadily nearer to that truth, by whose partial discovery I have been doomed to such a dreadful shipwreck; that man is not truly one but truly two'.[30]

If the literary background to Stevenson's Edinburgh was but a shadow of its former self, a relic which Stevenson may have admired but one which cast but little on his own career as a writer, then the fascination of that double self, so much part of the fabric of Edinburgh life, left a lasting impression on him. There was sufficient evidence to serve his purpose and to fire his imagination. Major Weir, the strict Covenanting soldier who was found to be a wizard; Deacon Brodie, respectable citizen by day, robber by night; Burke and Hare the body-snatchers with their resurrectionist confederate Dr Robert Knox; and Hogg's hall of mirrors and deception, the novel of demoniac possession, *The Private Memoirs and Confessions of a Justified Sinner*. All these were grist to the future writer's mill.

References

1 David Masson, *Edinburgh Sketches and Memories* (London 1892) 435.
2 Lord Cockburn, *Memorials of His Time*, ed. T. N. Foulis (Edinburgh 1910) 162.
3 Lady Holland, *Memoir* (London 1855) vol. 1, ch. 2.
4 Thomas Carlyle, *Reminiscences*, introd. Ian Campbell (London 1972) 317-18.
5 J. G. Lockhart, *Peter's Letters to His Kinfolk*, ed. William Ruddick (Edinburgh 1977) 97.
6 J. F. Ferrier, *Noctes Ambrosianae*, vol. 4 (Edinburgh 1885) 296.
7 ibid., 302.
8 Quoted in A. L. Strout, *The Life and Letters of James Hogg*, vol. 1 (Lubbock Texas 1946) 137.
9 *Abbotsford Notanda*, 146.
10 F. D. Tredrey, *The House of Blackwood* (Edinburgh 1954) 30.
11 Letter to Charles Baxter, Apia, 28 December 1889, in *RLS: Stevenson's Letters to Charles Baxter*, ed. DeLancey Ferguson and Marshall Waingrow (New Haven 1956) 253.
12 Letter to Charles Baxter, Vailima, 1 December 1892, in Ferguson and Waingrow, op. cit., 313-14.
13 Letter to Robert Louis Stevenson, Edinburgh, 20 January 1893, in Ferguson and Waingrow, op cit., 314, note 6.
14 W. M. Parker, *The House of Oliver and Boyd: A Record from 1778 to 1948*, unpublished typescript (Edinburgh Central Library 1963) 83.
15 David Masson, op. cit., 437.
16 William Power, *My Scotland* (Edinburgh 1934) 290.
17 Sir Arthur Conan Doyle, *The Firm of Girdlestone* (London 1890) 32.
18 Annie S. Swan, *My Life* (London 1934) 17.
19 ibid., 41.
20 Charles Dickens, *Morning Chronicle*, 18 September 1834.
21 Letter to Miss Laetitia Wheelwright, Haworth, 30 July 1850, quoted in Rosaline Masson, *In Praise of Edinburgh* (London 1912) 251.
22 Harriet Beecher Stowe, *Sunny Memories of Foreign Travel*, vol. 1 (London 1854) 37.
23 John Ruskin, *Lectures on Architecture and Painting* (London 1907) 2.
24 David Masson, op. cit., 359.
25 ibid., 429.
26 Robert Forsyth, *The Beauties of Scotland etc.* (Edinburgh 1805-08) vol. 1, 32.
27 Lord Cockburn, op. cit., 197.
28 ibid.

29 Robert Louis Stevenson and W. E. Henley, *Deacon Brodie* (Tusitala edition 1924) 19.
30 Robert Louis Stevenson, *Dr Jekyll and Mr Hyde* (London 1886) 109.

DOUGLAS GIFFORD

Stevenson and Scottish Fiction
The Importance of
The Master of Ballantrae

This essay argues the case for three main propositions. These propositions are interconnected; and if tenable, I think that their combined meanings allow *The Master of Ballantrae* to emerge as a fine and neglected Romantic and symbolic novel in the tradition of *Wuthering Heights* and *Moby Dick*; and the finest expression of Scottish fiction's deepest concerns in the nineteenth century.

My first proposition is that there existed from 1814 till 1914 a school of Scottish fiction with its own recurrent themes, and its own distinguishable symbolism. My second is that nearly all of Stevenson's Scottish fiction (and much of his total output of fiction) is mainly unsuccessful exploration of the almost obsessional material of his relations with his family and with Edinburgh bourgeois society and Scotland. *The Master of Ballantrae*, I suggest, is the clearest and most symbolic expression of his deepest tensions in these areas and thus of major importance in his output. The rest of the Scottish fiction is to be considered as 'trial runs' for it. Consequently I propose a reconsideration of the novel, defending its structure and contrasting and varied settings against previous attack, and emphasising the crucial and highly subtle use of the 'unreliable narrator', the prejudiced family retainer Mackellar. If, for example, we compare his function with that of Nellie Dean in *Wuthering Heights*, we can see that Stevenson's creation has the more complex and profound role. As a result, the novel can be seen as sharing in what amounts to a tendency in the Presbyterian and 'Puritan' novel towards mutually exclusive interpretations and sharp ambivalence. *The Master of Ballantrae* bears comparison with *The Scarlet Letter* or *Moby Dick* or *The Private Memoirs and Confessions of a Justified Sinner* in this respect.

The first area of discussion concerns that school of Scottish fiction of 1814–1914. I choose these dates, those of Scott's *Waverley* and John Macdougall Hay's *Gillespie* respectively, because these novels seem to me to enclose both the comparatively unbroken century of continuity in Scottish social and cultural life (a continuity to be shattered by the effects of the First World War) and the major Scottish novels which satirise what they see as the destructive and divisive social stereotypes that the century of continuity brings about, especially in nineteenth-century Scottish attitudes to self and family.

But within the century 1814–1914 there existed not just one but at least three schools of Scottish fiction, with the possibility of a fourth. There were two schools of 'escape' from the dreary realities which were transforming Scotland from a broadly rural and peasant nation to one of the most industrialised in the world; and it is worth recalling that hardly any novelist worthy of the name till Grassic Gibbon (in *Grey Granite* in 1934) thought fit to take as a subject the effects of massive industrial urbanisation on people from such very different previous backgrounds. Edwin Muir called our first school of Scottish fiction 'escape to Scotland'. This describes what we all recognise as a kind of fiction which survives even now. We need only work back from Nigel Tranter and Dorothy Dunnett, through Neil Munro and the more robust action novels of S. R. Crockett, past the work of James Grant and William Black and – to his discredit let it be said – the Stevenson of *The Black Arrow* and *St Ives* – to the more mechanical moving about of historical furniture of Walter Scott in *The Antiquary, Guy Mannering, Ivanhoe* and *The Talisman,* to realise the strength of a Scottish fiction which prefers to dress up what E. M. Forster called the 'And then... And then' type of narrative in historical guise.[1] The aim of such 'historical' fiction is in fact the opposite of historical, in that its central characters are familiar, ideal, and attractive to the modern reader, with the purpose of entertaining rather than illuminating the forces of real social change and their effect on society.

Our second kind of fiction of the period is often referred to as the Kailyard School of Scottish fiction. Here one enters more controversial ground – not as to what the school comprises, since most would accept that it has its hey-day in the work of J. M. Barrie, S. R. Crockett, Ian Maclaren and the like at the end of the nineteenth and beginning of the twentieth century. Controversy arises concerning two points: where the school begins and its final worth. Does the Kailyard originate with impulses to simplification and cliché which ante-date the novel, especially in poetry like that of Burns's 'Cottar's Saturday Night' and Hogg's 'Kilmeny'? Has Henry

Mackenzie's *The Man of Feeling* (1771) a hand in the shaping of such surrogate mythology? Has even Jeannie Deans, that 'cow-feeder's daughter' of indubitable virtue, some charge to answer here? These are scurrilous charges to many Scots; and they may find me even more scurrilous when I suggest that the Stevenson of *Weir of Hermiston,* in correspondence with S.R.Crockett as he wrote the novel, was already tainted with the Kailyard tendency to excessive sentimentality and distortion of the psychological true. Had I time enough I would enjoy trying to prove that *Weir* is a novel marred beyond redemption by the maudlin scenes of young Archie and Kirstie, a poor pair of children, 'playing the old game of falling in love'. 'Will I have met my fate?' wonders a Kirstie who seems to belong more to Crockett's *The Lilac Sunbonnet* than here, swallowing her sugar bool sweeties in church, and throughout chapter six making so many pretty little *People's Friend* changes of mood that shepherd-poet Dandie is driven to remark that 'at denner you were all sunshine and flowers and laughter, and now you're like the star of evening on a lake'![2] *Weir* has magnificent things in it, especially in the depiction of its demonic hanging judge jesting as he destroys the rags of self-respect of miserable Duncan Jopp. But it was becoming a Kailyard novel, and was besides far too mechanical in its laboured and anachronistic symbolism of the four black brothers who represent the hidden fire of Scottish peasantry, religion, poetry, and mechanical genius. Again, the Kailyard novel – and Stevenson's contribution to it, here and in novels like the nauseating piece of father-worship *The Misadventures of John Nicholson* or the indulgent pieces set in France like *The Treasure of Franchard* or *The Story of a Lie* – need not detain us long. Again, what we must acknowledge in leaving is that no less a critic than Francis Hart in his *The Scottish Novel* would take issue with all I have said, on the score that Scots are the last critics able to understand the true Edenic vision lying behind such redemptive fictions.[3] I accept the difference of opinion and pass on to our third, and most important, school of Scottish fiction.

We are left with two kinds of Scottish fiction to engage our serious critical attention. They are respectively a negative and satiric tradition of Romantic fiction and an affirmative, regenerative type which is only occasionally attempted by the major novelists – within our period, namely Scott, Stevenson and, less coherently, George Macdonald. And since, within our period, the attempts by these writers to portray in fiction the transcendence of Scottish limitations to social and personal development are less successful than their stronger and clearer satiric pictures of stagnating Scotland, we shall discuss their partial failure now, before considering the most significant recurrent type of Scottish fiction.

If I am granted for the moment what I have just suggested – that the strongest tradition is negative and satiric – then the fourth kind of Scottish fiction is the occasional attempt to create within such a framework a symbolic situation and eponymous hero within this situation representing Scotland regenerative. Scott tried this outstandingly in *Old Mortality* and *The Heart of Midlothian*, when in each case he created a situation where the sick forces of Scottish history in each novel were confronted by protagonists who drew their symbolic force from the fact that they represented 'nature's voice', and spoke for instinctive goodness of the heart such as Francis Hutcheson had argued for when he made the first utterances of the sentimental school of Scottish philosophy. My own liking and respect for Scott's work indeed relates to the extent to which he conscientiously tried from *Waverley* to *The Heart of Midlothian* to find the ideal figure to represent his case for liberal compromise and historical tolerance. Flora MacIvor, Henry Morton, and outstandingly, Jeannie Deans the cowfeeder's daughter, are the results in chronological and ascending order of that quest; and the fact that Flora fails because she is the reasonable woman identified with the unreasonable cause, that Morton fails because he cannot challenge the fact that it is not his idealism that wins the day but rather the Hanoverian and pragmatic settlement of 1689, and that Jeannie fails because her symbolic meaning as Heart of Midlothian and *Pilgrim's Progress* Mercy outweighs her naturalistic credibility, should not allow us to belittle Scott's genuine attempt to create a symbolic 'Condition of Scotland' novel. One admits his failure, as I think one must admit, for very different reasons, that of George Macdonald – and more important for our purposes, the failure in this respect of Stevenson.

And where does Stevenson ever attempt a novel of extended social comment on Scotland, with such a symbolic protagonist? I contend that this is to be found, broken-backed and inconclusive, but recognisable as such a transcendental attempt, in *Kidnapped* (1886) and *Catriona* (1893). The continuation of the adventures of David Balfour has long puzzled me. Indeed sustained length of treatment was always a problem for Stevenson – witness his *penchant* for the short tale, the series of related adventures, the novelette, and the number of unfinished tales. Sustained control of a large symbolic structure is not found often in his work, so it is all the more surprising that he should have felt, even after some time, that there was something unfinished, demanding resolution, in the matter of David Balfour. The questions this poses to us are three. First, what was there about David, of all his adolescent victim-heroes from the inept bourgeoisie of *The New Arabian Nights* and *The Dynamiter* to Jim Hawkins and Gordon Darnaway and John Nicholson, that made his actions different and worthy of further examination? Secondly, why suddenly decide to be ambitious of the long form when all previous work shows him happiest in the short story and novellette? And thirdly, what is there in *Catriona* which carries on, and relates to, the business of *Kidnapped*? It is true that David at the outset of *Kidnapped* seems to be another of those adolescents whose lives are to be ravaged by Chance, a recurrent and signficant theme of the Stevenson who must frequently have felt that Chance was indeed the only factor which could liberate him from the suffocating restrictions of parental love and disapproval. Chance saves David's life at the top of the stairs of the House of Shaws; Chance steers Alan Breck, his *alter ego*, into his life. But – as we know from the letters – Stevenson's problems with David grew, and the character deepened and changed. Indeed, David and Alan Breck moved towards the positions of Henry and James Ballantrae, as they evolved towards a juxtaposition of dour Calvinist-derived commonsense and rigid moral earnestness and extrovert romantic-Celtic waywardness of imagination and emotion. But more important than this shadowy anticipation of the oppositions of *Ballantrae* and *Weir of Hermiston* is the fact that David is *not* to be contained within adolescent guidelines or within limits as foil to Alan Breck. He rapidly becomes *the* moral agent of the book, haunted by the tears of James of the Glen's wife, perceptive to the good (in a manner reminiscent of Jeannie Deans) even in his captors Hoseason and the ship's doctor. I suggest that in David, Stevenson makes the change from protagonist as adolescent victim of Chance adventure to protagonist as moral agent and witness in the manner of Henry Morton and Jeannie Deans. Why then continue his adventures into *Catriona*, especially when the major business of *Kidnapped* seems to be settled? His inheritance is assured, Alan Breck has escaped. What remains unsettled is an issue raised half-way through *Kidnapped*, an issue which I suggest is the first to engage David's new moral awareness, and an issue which – quite apart from Catriona herself – will form the major part of the novel *Catriona*. David witnessed the murder of the Red Fox, Campbell of Glenure. The second part of

Kidnapped and the first part of *Catriona* are Stevenson's attempts to create a *Heart of Midlothian* novel of Scottish social regeneration. The fact that he fails should not blind us to the epic scale of his attempt. David, like Jeannie or Morton, is 'nature's voice', the suffering conscience of a 'grass roots' Scotland who, like them, sees about him in Prestongrange, in the corrupt legal system, in the ubiquitous expediency and social hypocrisy, a debased modern Scotland. Against this, like them, he pits his honesty, courage, instinctive sense of right. Alan refers to him as the queerest and most unique creature in Scotland; and, in a manner significantly close to that of Jeannie Deans, his journeys have symbolic force. (It is also significant that *Catriona* makes mention of the Porteous affair of *The Heart*, as well as the Wildfire Rocks and a strangely un-Stevensonian and prophetic hag who foresees the gallows beneath blackening bodies.) Like Jeannie, David comes from the country and humble background of Scotland. His journey, from Leith to the Orkneys to the West, *surrounds* Scotland, sampling Highland and Lowland culture, winning, like Jeannie, strange allies from whom he elicits reluctant goodness. Unlike Jeannie, he fails. His Bass Rock captivity represents the difference between Scott and Stevenson. James of the Glens is hung, and the first part of *Catriona* ends with what I read as a crucial abdication on Stevenson's part from involvement in 'the condition of Scotland'.

> So there was the final upshot of my politics! Innocent men
> have perished before James, and are like to keep on perishing
> (in spite of all our wisdom) till the end of time. And till the
> end of time young folk (who are not yet used with the duplicity
> of life or men) will struggle as I did, and make heroical
> resolves, and take long risks; and the course of events will
> push them upon the one side and go on like a marching army.
> James was hanged; and here was I dwelling in the house of
> Prestongrange, and grateful to him for his fatherly attention...
> and the villains of that plot were decent, kind, respectable
> fathers of families, who went to kirk and took the sacrament!
>
> But I had had my view of that detestable business they call
> politics – I had seen it from behind, when it is all bones and
> blackness; and I was cured for life . . . A plain, quiet path, was
> that which I was ambitious to walk in, when I might keep my
> head out of the way of dangers and my conscience out of the
> road of temptation. For, upon a retrospect, it appeared I had
> not done so grandly, after all; but with the greatest possible
> amount of big speech and preparation, had accomplished

nothing.[4]

The quote is long, because it is so important. Once again I discover, in part two, in the overdone and often maudlin relations of the shy lovers David and Catriona in Holland, that unfortunate later tendency of Stevenson towards Crockett and Barrie and the Kailyard which I suggest would have spoiled even *Weir of Hermiston*. The quote above marks his typical unwillingness to confront and his inability to defeat the bourgeois values of father (that 'fatherly attention' of Prestongrange is so revealing!) and respectable Edinburgh. It's significant that his most bitter remarks on 'decent, kind, respectable . . . families' has to be distanced and disguised in this and other fiction like *Weir* or *Dr Jekyll and Mr Hyde*.

Stevenson avoided the full task of evaluating his Scottish background. Does it then follow that we must position his work beneath that of Hogg or Scott, or in the present, Gunn or Gibbon? I think not. There still existed one tradition of Scottish fiction which could help him to genuine and full creativity – that of Scott's *Waverley* or *Redgauntlet*, of Galt's *The Entail*, and, to a lesser extent, of Hogg's *The Justified Sinner*. In *The Master of Ballantrae* Stevenson was to take this tradition and create its archetype.

What is this tradition and how is it recognisably different from, say, that of *Wuthering Heights*, or, at the end of the century, *The Mayor of Casterbridge*, both of which, in respect of use of landscape, or demonic local tyrants, resemble the Scottish novels?

Francis Hart in *The Scottish Novel* prefers other types of classification, which have their own validity but seem to me to avoid the outstanding tradition, which one critic, writing of George Douglas Brown's *The House with the Green Shutters*, described in poetry as having as its object the desire to

Paint village hell where sadist monster mutters
Till Scotland's one mad House with the Green Shutters
Depict the lust that lurks in hall and hovel
And build thereon a Scottish national novel.[5]

But the emphasis here on a kind of crude realism, endorsed by Angus McDonald when he quoted the poem, should not blind us to the fact that the tradition is essentially Romantic and symbolic. David Daiches went some way in identifying the polarities and their significance in his pioneer essay on 'Scott's achievement as a novelist', when he stressed that Scott's typical pattern of opposition placed Past against Present, Order against Disorder, and – very broadly – a cause of the Heart against a cause of the Head. Scott nearly always in his Scottish fiction chooses a period of civil disruption which presents such a possible pattern; but I would allege that the pattern of Scott is the base pattern for the serious and satiric Scottish novelist of the next century following *Waverley* in 1814.

The recurrent themes of nineteenth-century Scottish fiction of this kind are those of the divided self; the divided family which contains the broken self; the divided nation behind the fragmented family. Morbid states of psychology as frequent focal points of the fiction were recognised as early as 1933 by Kitchin;[6] and the converse of this, the use of a 'transitional devil simile', as Coleman Parsons calls it,[7] which is related to but not at all identical with the demonic and Byronic element in the work of the Brontës, becomes something of a *sine qua non* of the tradition. And here I would go further than Daiches or Kitchin and tentatively suggest that, taking the conclusions of Muir in his study *Scott and Scotland* (of the first part) one can derive a meaning from the recurrent pattern which is in its intensity and kind unique to the Scottish novel. Muir argued his 'dissociation of sensibility' theory in the first part of that study.[8] He suggested that the organic and whole culture of pre-1560 and the Reformation suffered separation into mutually exclusive parts; that emotion, as linked with the older Scottish language, was separated from thought, and consequently, when emotion and thought were thus separated, emotion became irresponsible and thought became arid; and if one felt in Scots and thought in English, one's feelings and expression of feeling in Scots would be likely to be self-indulgent and one's thoughts and expression of them somewhat arid.

I find it poignant and regrettable that Muir failed to apply the implications of this theory to the matter of his study, to Scott. Possibly dissociated by this time from Scotland himself, Muir failed to see that Scott did not always suffer a failure of creative and critical awareness. He further failed to see that Hogg, Galt, Stevenson, Brown and MacDougall Hay – to leave out Muir's contemporaries, Gibbon, Gunn and MacColla – did not fall victim to the divisive and degenerative forces of Scottish Materialism, Grundyism, and sentimental Romanticisation, but rather used them as materials for satire and exposure, albeit in apparently anachronistic guise. Thus *Waverley* satirises a central mentality which suffers 'tartan fever'; its central motif is that of the delusive dream, its reductive image of the highlands the 'bra' Highlander tat's painted on the board afore the change-house they ca' Lucky Middlemass's'. Waverley is caught between irresponsible and yet obsessively

greedy Highlanders, disorderly and deluded, and excessively
mechanistic, depressingly orderly bourgeois systems represented
by the merchants of Dundee and the unimaginative disciplines of
the Hanoverian army, which Waverley finds impossibly stifling.
The pattern is that of *Rob Roy*; and Rob Roy, cause of the Past,
representative of the Scottish Outlaw Myth, Jacobite sympathiser,
is blood cousin to Baillie Nicol Jarvie, canny merchant who wel-
comes the road 'West awa' yonder' to sugar, tea and tobacco from
the American colonies, basis of Glasgow's flourishing. Scott tells
us that Scotland has become the battlefield of the Heart and the
Head. We may dislike his compromise solutions, but his satiric
vision outstrips his rational suggestion for regeneration, just as his
wonderful picture of the sick heart of Midlothian outstrips his
naive pictures of Jeannie Deans making all well on the island (sic!)
of Roseneath.

Hogg's *Sinner* does not fit so easily into this pattern, although
related. Hogg's opposition there is of older, healthier, tougher
Scotland as represented by the laird of Dalcastle against a sick
modern evangelical religious consciousness. The Shepherd of Ettrick mourned in all his fiction a simpler Scottish transition, that of
rural community with oral tradition of ballad and story giving way
to a Scotland sick either through religion or social snobbery. But
his Robert Wringhim looks forward to Henry Jekyll and, above all,
Ephraim Mackellar, who destroys his firstborn son in pursuit of his
materialist dream, anticipates Weir and more especially the brutal
merchant figures John Gourlay and Gillespie Strang. John Speirs
noted that Douglas Brown had put 'the nineteenth century in
allegory' in *Green Shutters*.[9] Again, I'd go further, and suggest that
the novel, like its relatives, is symbolic; that Gourlay represents
Scottish greed, Scottish elimination of the gentler virtues and arts
from its educational and social systems, that his devilish nature and
stature represent the degeneration of wholeness and goodness in
Scottish life. And the pattern is borne out in the placing, in all these
novels, of a son (usually of the very same name as the father, in
order to suggest that they are the parts of what should be a whole)
who has, possibly to excess, the gentler virtues. Archie Weir's
'shivering delicacy' and 'splairging' are close to young John Gourlay's 'splurging' and hypersensitivity; Eochan Strang is their de-
scendent and stands in exactly the same relation to his brutal father
Gillespie.

Indeed, father-son opposition became the standard opposition of
symbolic forces in the Scottish novel, with Gibbon and Gunn and

even A. J. Cronin in *Hatter's Castle* using it occasionally as stereo-type. What is fascinating is that Muir did not see that a novel such as *The Green Shutters* perfectly substantiated his theory of dissocia-tion. If this be doubted, read the crucial central episode of the novel, when young John Gourlay tries for the Raeburn essay prize at Edinburgh University. Gaspy little sentences, vivid fragments of sense-impressions of an Arctic Night, are all he can manage. His professor makes extensive comment on both the talent, which captures the feeling of the thing, and its dangers. With *thought*, he says, and hard work, such a talent for pure feeling may become higher and consecrative – but without thought, dissociated from it, it would simply be a curse. Gourlay ignores the advice, and the House of Gourlay is destroyed. In *Latitudes* Muir discussed the novel – and failed to remember and to apply to it the very theory which lay at the heart of *Scott and Scotland*.[10] And if a critic like Muir could miss the deeper meanings of Brown's novel, it is not surprising that he and critics of Stevenson should miss the deeper meanings of *The Master of Ballantrae*.

I come now to my second proposition, that nearly all of Steven-son's Scottish fiction is mainly unsuccessful exploration of his personal relations with family, Edinburgh, and Scotland. No-one now would dispute that Stevenson's relations with his family, especially his father, produced deep tensions and guilts throughout his life. But it is not the finer points of biographical truth that matter too much. We need not explore too far the extent to which Stevenson took his youthful rebellions. This is less important than the evidence of the range of the stories that, out of this area of confused values, 'sad little mutinies', love and hate, came equally confused statements of ever-changing moral stance.

Simplifying Edwin Eigner's more ambitious and far more subtle groupings of Stevenson's stories,[11] it seems to me that the most useful starting point for an understanding of most of Stevenson's fiction is that of his moral ambivalence. Nearly all his stories, with the exception of the more straightforward tales of supernatural tradition such as 'The Bodysnatcher' or 'Tod Lapraik' move be-tween two opposite poles of morality. Up till David Balfour nearly all his protagonists are adolescents confused about moral value. Although the earliest of these, the rather helpless middle class youths of *The New Arabian Nights* and *The Dynamiter* (1885) seem to move in the singularly amoral world of the exotic Prince Florizel (Mr T. Godall), that device of escape to adventure land is quickly ended. The later adolescents, from François Villon in 'A

Lodging for the Night', to 'Will o' the Mill' to Denis de Boileau in 'The Sire de Malatroit's Door' live in a confused but singularly moral world. They have choices to make, values to declare. And what is outstanding is that they all choose differently. Stevenson can make none of them speak authoritatively and confidently for a fixed moral vision. Villon is the demonic adolescent who spares the kindly father figure; Denis is the innocent adolescent who is coerced into marriage by the devilish aristocrat Malatroit. Two youngsters, two father-figures; and their crossover of positions represents what happens in all Stevenson's fiction. In *The Misadventures of John Nicholson* a relationship between son and father repeats, with variation, the polarisation of 'A Lodging for the Night', with the settled middle-class father this time accepting (with nauseating Goodness) the capitulation of his prodigal son. One juxtaposes this with the transposed situation of *Weir of Hermiston*, where the student freethinking of Archie leads to a real compassion for his fellow humans which is revolted by the demonic and jesting insensitivity of his respectable Edinburgh father.

But, as Eigner noticed, Stevenson didn't often use an actual father-son confrontation.[12] Instead that confrontation is expressed in dualisms and pairings of contrasted characters. Frequently there is an adolescent witness to this, as with Jim Hawkins and his positioning between the world of the Liveseys and Trelawneys, Doctor and Squire, and the world of Long John Silver. The earlier part of *Kidnapped* shows this situation. Or, moving on to the point of respectable maturity as starting point, Dr Jekyll is shown as deliberately separating and indulging those parts of his nature which he regards as evil, in a personality akin to Villon or Silver. I do not say that Stevenson always rings such changes. Sometimes both kinds of protagonists – and the element of demonism – are rigidly controlled, as in 'Will o' the Mill', where Will is neither son or father, but evader of all struggle – and the Devil is thus watered down to a kindly Death Figure, who peacefully takes the aging but unaged Will (literally an uncommitted Will?) from a strangely unreal Neverland. Alternatively, Stevenson presents a story within a traditional type, such as the Gothic-Christian 'Markheim', or as in the Scottish traditional supernatural tales like 'Thrawn Janet' or 'The Merry Men'. The latter owes something too to Melville in its use of Puritan ambivalence and sea symbolism. But even in these stories one can detect a developing trait of Stevenson's work which *The Master of Ballantrae* will bring to fruition; namely that ambiguity which had, admittedly, been the hallmark of the traditional

Burns-Hogg-Scott supernatural tale – but which was in Stevenson's hands to become a metaphor for something much deeper.

Thus, by the time he came to write *The Master of Ballantrae*, Stevenson had exhibited throughout his fiction two traits which were closely connected to his tortuous relations with his father and family background. The first trait led him to create perpetually in pairings or opposites – Prince Florizel and his dependant simple young men, Villon and his fatherly burgher, Frank Cassilis and his dour friend Northmour in *A Pavilion on the Links*, Jekyll and Hyde, Balfour and Breck. The second trait led him increasingly to deal with these or his other worlds with ambivalence, allowing neither of the groups, their values, or even the worlds of rationalism or the supernatural to have a final indubitable value.

Tentatively I suggest that two dominating concepts for Stevenson in the years around his father's death (1887) emerged in the ideas of 'Providence' and 'Chance'. 'Chance' had always played a significant role in his creations, dropping his inexperienced young men into worlds completely different from the settled, traditionally structured worlds of their parental background, amongst mad bombers, suicide clubs, exiled Bohemian princes of supernatural capabilities, treasure islands, lonely Hebridean bays with sunken galleons, and marriages with the beautiful daughters of devilish French aristocrats. Understandably it attracted Stevenson as an amoral 'way out' of his own dilemma of values, and thus became a fictional device for releasing himself and his protagonists from the weight of moral choice. But I feel that to the maturing Stevenson 'Chance' as a concept became something deeper, truer to the life of the later nineteenth century. By the time of *The Master of Ballantrae* it had become the sign of a way of life opposite to that represented by 'Providence', the force behind the world of Thomas Stevenson and Presbyterian Edinburgh. More clearly than ever before, Stevenson bases one Master of Ballantrae, Henry, in a world of 'Providence'; and the other Master of Ballantrae, James, in a secular, and, as one critic has called it, 'ur-existential', world of 'Chance' where his making of decisions on the basis of coin-tossing reflects his 'belief' in a random universe – and his disbelief in conventional morality or Mackellar's 'Providence'.[13]

It is crucial to my reconsideration of *The Master of Ballantrae* that we consider and continue to accept what most readers would initially agree is a fair reading of the novel. Such a reading would accept that in Mackellar we have a reliable witness to the fortunes of the house of Durrisdeer. He may be a somewhat pernickety, spinsterish Presbyterian of the old school, but in many ways such dry traits supply that very credibility which the reader so instinctively seeks in tracing the rights and wrongs of the various Durrisdeers. It is part of Stevenson's great skill that Mackellar supplies, effortlessly, this reader's need – in something resembling the way Nellie Dean answers a need in *Wuthering Heights*. Incredible and unnatural events are made palatable in both by being anchored to' acceptable and reassuring figures of social certainty.

In this reading Henry becomes victim of history and James. Time has placed him in an inferior role; fate has given him less obvious gifts than James, less attractive to the neighbourhood and to Alison and his father. And what more likely than that the quieter brother to a charismatic and subtle extrovert should retreat somewhat within himself, repressing and denying through mingled stubbornness and jealousy the qualities which might rival those of his brother? Read like this, Henry's story is a painful tracing of misunderstanding and deliberate misdirection by James, whereby Alison's, their father's, and the world's view of Henry is belittled by Henry's reticence, bad luck, and James's guileful Art. In this reading the kinship of Henry to David Balfour stands out clearly, their mutual reserve actually adding to our liking for them, the underdogs of a world which prefers the superficial charm of a Breck or James Ballantrae.

Clearly, too, in this interpretation, James's is a study of evil. Black is his colour in dress and in image or association, from that 'very black mark' against him in the opening pages to the night settings that surround his most mysterious episodes. The transition from this motif of blackness to the imputation of demonic traits is effortless, from his childhood exploits when he masquerades against Wullie White the Wabster as Auld Hornie, or his father cries 'I think you are a devil of a son to me', to when he takes command of pirate Teach's ship 'little Hell', or later, when he appears as Satan in Milton's epic, a fallen angel. (We recall that Stevenson's 'editor' in his Preface remembered that a Durrisdeer 'had some strange passages with the devil'.) Most important is James's artfulness; one recalls that the Devil himself was Father of Lies, and James is in this respect very much a disciple, since he is utter master of the lie unstated, the contrived situation where he will affect a person or company with a gesture, an argument, or a song, theatrically and consummately presented. 'I never yet failed to charm a person when I wanted', he says to Mackellar at the end of the voyage on the *Nonesuch*, when even Mackellar admitted that

James and he had come to live together on excellent terms. Taken this way, James is the *incubus*, the descendant of Hogg's Gilmartin, who haunts his brother as George Dalcastle was haunted in *The Justified Sinner*.

And taken this way the novel is a tragedy, whereby Henry, having been all but destroyed by this malevolent quasi-devil, completes his own and his family's destruction by descending to the dark levels of his brother; so much so that the running devil-motif comes in the closing stages to apply to Henry, and Henry's dealings become every bit as immoral and with even nastier people than James's or his colleagues'.

But I can never remember being happy with this reading. Even as youthful reader I could never understand how James, that supernaturally quick athlete of catlike reflexes and endless experience in the world's wildest scenes of action, could ever have lost the duel with his brother. For all the argument of 'contained and glowing fury', for all I had sympathy for Henry and anger against James for what he had done to him, it seemed even then too 'Boy's Own' a solution to suggest that sheer right welled up in depressed, cheated, deprived Henry at just the necessary moment. And, as I came to later Stevenson criticism, these feelings grew more acute. The narrators of the action, Mackellar and Chevalier Burke, changed too awkwardly, with little point; the locations changed too arbitrarily, too wildly from rain-gloomy Scotland to swamp-dank Albany or strange sea-voyages; poetic justice had been lost by reducing Henry's goodness to something so inconsequential that he was allowed to share the same grave as his devil-brother. Most damning consideration of all was that Stevenson committed the final artistic sin of changing his vision in mid-stream, having Henry reborn after the duel as a malevolent adult-child, crippled by guilt and warped into a new shape which increasingly rivalled the degradation of James.

I now argue that Stevenson wished only to allow this reading to exist *as a possibility*. With the example of Hogg's *Sinner* before him of 'reversible interpretation', with indeed the tendency of the Presbyterian and Puritan traditions in poetry and fiction towards alternative meanings familiar to him from examples as diverse as Burns's 'Tam o' Shanter' to Hawthorne's 'Young Goodman Brown' and *The Scarlet Letter*, Melville's *Moby-Dick*, and even his friend James's *The Portrait of a Lady* published some eight years earlier, there were many attractions towards a fiction of mutually exclusive interpretations. And the greatest of these attractions, I submit, would lie in the fact that such ambiguity would release Stevenson from all his previous need to struggle confusedly with emblems of a shifting moral consciousness. *The Master of Ballantrae* derives its greatness from the fact that it is the only novel of Stevenson's successfully to resolve – even although it is by sidestep and sleight of creative hand – the dilemma of values so manifest in the other fiction. This is not all. In solving his own problem of values by creating a novel which in effect has no definitive value structure at all, Stevenson created the classic version of the Scottish 'dissociation of sensibility' novel.

This, however, is to beg the question of Stevenson's other meaning for the novel. There are, after all, two Masters of Ballantrae. The very title poses a question similar to that of James in *The Portrait of a Lady*. It warns us, since it does not name the identity of the Master, of a struggle of brothers and opposed 'moralities'. And in this struggle, sensitive reading will show that from the very beginning Henry is not that symbol of undoubted worth that the first reading presupposes. From that first unnecessary 'You know very well that you are the favourite' when quarrelling with James, there is revealed something petulant and small in his personality. He is 'strangely obstinate' in silence when his true nature is misunderstood, and early we are told that he's 'neither very bad nor very able, but an honest, solid sort of lad'. Whatever else, he is certainly a dogged stay-at-home, emotionally – at least to the observer – a rather arid fellow, willing in the end to marry for the pity of the lady who loves his brother, 'by nature inclining to the parsimonious'. 'The weakness of my ground', he tells Mackellar, 'lies in myself, that I am not one who engages love'. When he is ill his instinctive preference for business emerges, 'mortifying' even Mackellar with 'affairs, cyphering figures, and holding disputation with the tenantry'.

But Stevenson is far too subtle to underdraw Henry to the point of symbolic simplicity. One of the most moving glimpses of the novel is of Henry, early on, doing the accounts of Durrisdeer with Mackellar, and falling into a deep muse, staring straight west into the sun over the long sands, where the freetraders, with a great force of men and horses, were scouring on the beach. Mackellar marvels that Henry is not blinded; Henry frowns, rubs his brow, smiles and says: 'You would not guess what I was thinking . . . I was thinking I would be a happier man if I could ride and run the danger of my life, with these lawless companions.' Like James? Henry's tragedy is deepened by the fact that he knows his own malformation, and he knows that he cannot be what he is not. His trade is far from free, he recognises, as he tells Mackellar 'and with that we may get back to our accounts'.

The episode has however made us early aware of depths of rebellious feeling in Henry. Foreshortened emotions have their revenges, and Stevenson most effectively will show Henry's emerging in catastrophic fashion at the duel, and then, since guilt will refashion the man anew, emerging in yet more poisoned manner. After the duel, 'something of the child he exhibited; a cheerfulness quite foreign to his previous character'. This good humour is false, based as it is on brain-damaged forgetfulness, implying that Henry cannot face the reality of his actions. He beats the groom, which is 'out of all his former practice'; has 'a singular furtive smile'; and utters his black curse on James – 'I wish he was in hell', in front of his son – which reveals how far the disease has gone in de-Christianising him. Out of dissociation of personality comes what looks very like evil, as he poisons his son's mind, and insists on his title as Master – 'the which he was punctilious in exacting'. Need I follow his further deterioration? His psycho-somatic degradation, as his body grows slack, stooping, walking with a running motion? By the end, in his employment of the dregs of Albany cut-throats to do away with James, he has paralleled if not outdone James's most suspect deeds.

If further evidence is needed that Stevenson early warns us to be on our guard against too facile moral appraisal of the brothers, consider how subtly he arranges their background and support. At first only Mackellar supports Henry, with one crucial exception. In chapter one, beyond the family, 'there was never a good word for Mr Henry', except for Macconochie, 'an old, ill-spoken, swearing, ranting, drunken dog'. On James's side, John Paul, 'a little, bald, solemn, stomachy man, a great professor of piety . . .'; and, says Mackellar, 'I have often thought it an odd circumstance in human nature that these two serving men should each have been the champion of his contrary, and made light of their own virtues when they beheld them in a master'. Here is dissociation with a vengeance! Here is warning that strange compensations must be paid when whole critical and emotional awareness is lost. For beyond this lies a pattern of similar waywardness. The country opinion is never reliable. James becomes a false hero after the presumption of his death in the Rebellion, Jessie Broun unnaturally swinging against her former helper, Henry, and crying up her betrayer James as a saint. Can we then trust the picture when, in mirror image,

James is isolated with Secundra Dass against a hostile Albany?

We come to the question at the heart of my discussion. And it is a question of *pattern*. Were we to give visual expression to the shape of our novel, it would resemble that of *Vanity Fair*, in that the fortunes of the principal pair of characters would complete two opposed rising and falling movements. Like the opposed nadirs and zeniths of Becky and Amelia, those of Henry and James would appear so:

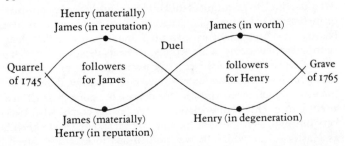

Henry (materially)
James (in reputation)

James (in worth)

Duel

Quarrel of 1745

followers for James

followers for Henry

Grave of 1765

James (materially)
Henry (in reputation)

Henry (in degeneration)

The comparison with Thackeray breaks down on closer inspection, however. The first movement, up to the duel, has as its theme (in this interpretation) the temporary triumph of Henry's appearance over his reality, while the second movement is not in fact a reversal of this so much as the restatement of a further riddle. And the answer to this riddle is dependant on the fulcrum of the entire novel, and the most brilliant device Stevenson ever employed. The answer to this novel's meaning lies with the character of Mackellar, who has influenced his changing pattern, at times decisively, as when he translates Alison from James's camp to Henry's with his carefully prepared dossier of letters which tell against James.

Why, virtually alone amongst his adolescent raconteurs, did Mackellar emerge as Stevenson's 'mouthpiece' now? Why did he decide to tell the tale through such an 'unrelated' persona? Was it simply to give him the credibility of Utterson the lawyer or Dr Lanyon of *Jekyll*, the reliability of Rankeillor in *Kidnapped*? If this is the reason, why then include so many examples of Mackellar's own prejudices and defects of character? Not only is he 'squaretoes' to the exuberant free-traders, he is an 'old maid' to Alison, who accuses him of never ceasing to meddle in the House affairs. He is a 'devil of a soldier in the steward's room at Durrisdeer', by the tenants' report, and he, like Henry, has never attracted love – far less risked marriage. He actively dislikes women.[14]

I suggest that Stevenson was working in the tradition of the dramatic monologue; and this is a genre with a very strong set of Scottish roots which would be known to Stevenson. From Alan Ramsay's 'Last Words of Lucky Spence' to Burns's 'Holy Willie's Prayer'; from Hogg's 'Sinner's Account' in *The Justified Sinner* to Galt's fictional monologues of minister, provost, and Covenanting Avenger (in *Ringan Gilhaize*), the Scottish tradition of self-revealing, unintentionally self-satiric monologue is as strong as any Stevenson could find, say, in contemporary work like Browning's 'My Last Duchess'. Indeed, Mackellar springs into vivid black-and-white relief if one envisages him as a later Holy Willie or Robert Wringhim.

As basis then for my second interpretation, let us examine Mackellar in a little depth. And, as he is always insisting on chapter and verse, 'like a witness in a court' (a favourite device of Mackellar's, this presentation of apparently inconfutable detail, *as though* he is presenting a meticulous case) let us insist on examining his evidence as though it were being submitted to strict lawyerly scrutiny. For example, just what exactly is that 'very black mark' against James's name which Mackellar brings up in the opening pages? Mackellar, after mentioning the accusation, as we decide our basic loyalties, goes on, 'but the matter was hushed up at the time, and so defaced by legends before I came into these parts, that I scruple to set it down. If it was true, it was a horrid fact in one so young; and if false, it was a horrid calumny'.[15] Indeed, Mackellar lists as one of the Master's crimes that of his treatment of Jessie Broun. Are we to hear Stevenson endorsing this? Would more liberal questioning establish a picture of wild oats and stuffy disapproval? And as to the opening wilfulness of James's insistence on going out in the Rebellion – does not the blame finally rest with the weak father, the Master of Ballantrae of the time, who failed to act with authority? Mackellar displays his prejudice at every turn. One remembers his disapproval of James's reading matter (and his lace); 'Caesar's "Commentaries", . . . Hobbes . . . Voltaire, a book upon the Indies, one on the mathematics, far beyond where I have studied.'

But once suspected, examples of Mackellar's unreliability abound. I want to focus on four issues as crucial to the development of our acceptance or not of his word. They are the matters of the duel, of the dossier of spy papers concocted for Alison, the *Nonesuch* Voyage, and James's reception at Albany.

I have already indicated my unease concerning the outcome of the duel. We must remember that the most serious allegations of cowardly treachery are about to be made concerning James. All we have to go on is Mackellar's account. But if this is so, must we not take the account in *all* its parts? Including the preparations for the duel, when Mackellar told the brothers that he would prevent it?

> And now here is a blot upon my life. At these words of mine the Master turned his blade against my bosom; I saw the light run along the steel; and I threw up my arms and fell to my knees before him on the floor. 'No, no,' I cried, like a baby.
>
> 'We shall have no more trouble with him,' said the Master. 'It is a good thing to have a coward in the house.'[16]

Mackellar's reliability would seem at the very least to be impaired by his emotional instability. And now we have the duel itself.

> I am no judge of the play; my head, besides, was gone with cold and fear and horror; but it seems that Mr Henry took and kept the upper hand from the engagement, crowding in upon his foe with a contained and glowing fury. Nearer and nearer he crept upon the man, till of a sudden the Master leaped back with a little sobbing oath; and I believe the movement brought the light once more against his eyes. To it they went again on the fresh ground; but now methought closer, Mr Henry pressing more outrageously, the Master beyond doubt with shaken confidence. For it is beyond doubt he now recognised himself for lost, and had some taste of the cold agony of fear; or he had never attempted the foul stroke. I cannot say I followed it, my untrained eye was never quick enough to seize details, but it appears he caught his brother's blade . . . .[17]

I submit this long quote as a superb example of Stevenson's crafty duplicity of intention. Notice especially the arrangement of 'I am no judge', 'I believe', 'it seems', 'methought' and the like in contrast to the more typical Mackellar factual terseness, 'for it is beyond doubt' (twice), 'certainly Mr Henry only saved himself by leaping'. Would not any defence lawyer for James demolish the credibility of this account in very little time, on the basis that it argued first for essential limitations of subjectivity, and then proceeded to assert the validity of these subjective (and prejudiced) impressions?

Moving to the later business of the spy dossier we are yet again presented by Stevenson with crafty duplicity of purpose. On the face of it the four types of letter submitted to Alison in 1757 appear a fair and damning 'schedule', as Mackellar imposingly calls them, especially in the fourth type, the letters between James and the British Under-Secretary of State, which most effectively show James to have run with the hare and the hounds. There are two qualifying factors, however. The first is Mackellar's unholy glee at his find in raiding the Master's papers – 'I rubbed my hands, I sang aloud in my glee. Day found me at the pleasing task'. One realises, too, that Alison, affected as she is by the dossier's toppling of James from his romantic pedestal, perceives what Mackellar does not, that the dossier is 'a sword of paper' against him. 'Papers or no papers, the door of this house stands open for him; he is the rightful heir.' Even more important is the question of James's guilt and treachery. I would now re-emphasize that the entire novel is based on a piece of duplicity; namely, the fact that the house of Ballantrae (like many others of the day) chose to solve the delicate problem of sending one son out with the Jacobites and keeping another at home as loyal to the established Crown. All were privy to this; Mackellar censures it not. Now recall the date of the submission of the dossier: 1757. The 'spy' letters ran from three years previously; that is, from 1754, almost ten years after the collapse of Charles's cause. By 1754, and with Charles increasingly the hopeless toper of Europe, are we to blame James for doing what his family had in 1745 condoned? It surely is a bit premature to ostracise James because Mackellar tells us he wrote to the 'English Secretary' (elsewhere *Under*-secretary) concerning what we are not in a position to know.

I must at this point, before being accused of overprotest concerning Mackellar, remind the reader that I also completely allow that James *is* a spy, that – according to another interpretation – Mackellar is utterly reliable. But, whatever his reliability in that interpretation, there is no question that, given greater exposure to James, his entire tone and relationship with James changes. Can this not be read as showing that, when the conditions for prejudice are changed, Mackellar also changes his judgements? Once again his credibility is in doubt, and nothing so damages his case as the *Nonesuch* voyage.

Warnings reminiscent of those surrounding Melville's *Pequod* abound; the ship is as rotten as a cheese, she is on what should be her last voyage. As these accumulate, we become aware that the ship is correlative to Mackellar's own strange guilty feelings. He suffers from 'a blackness of spirit'; he is poisoned as never before in soul and body, although he freely confesses that the master shows him a fair example of forbearance. Mackellar again denounces the Master's taste and style in reading (Richardson's *Clarissa*); and excels himself when he prays during the storm for the foundering and loss of the ship and all her crew, as long as the Master should thus be destroyed. Again the language indicates the disease within Mackellar. 'The thought of the man's death . . . took possession of my mind. I hugged it, I found it sweet in my belly', he tells us in a tone exactly like Robert Wringhim's. Ironically, the captain thanks him for saving the ship through prayer! Then follows his murder attempt on the Master, who (with that uncanny reflex swiftness that was his at all points but that of the duel) both escapes and pardons, in the fullest fashion, his would-be assassin. We must return briefly to the *Nonesuch* in a moment. Let me round off my four issues concerning Mackellar by pointing out that when James does arrive in Albany, he is accused of murder. In fact James is in this case guilty of nothing more than trying to cure his 'victim', young Chew. Mackellar will later learn of his innocence in this matter from the Chevalier Burke; but Mackellar refuses to correct the record, allowing yet another 'very black mark' to be stacked against his enemy. And in the closing sequences we see Mackellar condemning the fratricidal plans of Henry, but destroying his own moral validity by refusing to separate himself from Henry's cause.

We are left, in this interpretation, with a startling thought. Allowing that Secundra Dass, the mysterious Indian, is James's personal 'familiar', must we not begin to suspect that Henry is accompanied by his? One remembers that Mackellar is 'a devil of a steward'; he too dresses in black; and goes on board the *Nonesuch* 'as the devil would have it'. Once again our Devil metaphor makes a transition, and we look upon events in a different light.

After all, James, as Alison pointed out, is the rightful heir. What young man of spirit would not identify with the romantic cause of Prince Charles? Is it so improbable that a young man (James was not yet 24 in 1745) of imagination and passion should go the way in Paris of the aristocratic youth Burns describes in 'The Twa Dogs' as parading at operas and stews? That is, we admit that he was indeed a wild young man, but to deny that there was anything so devilish in his conduct? No-one doubts his courage or resourcefulness. And it is important to distinguish between James the younger and James on his return after the duel. James the younger was a spendthrift. The greatest amount of sympathy we can accord him then relates to the fact that when he returns he finds Mackellar and Henry orga-nised against him, and that the woman who loves him is unavail-able to him. But his second return is different. Even Mackellar admits this. In contrast to Henry, fattening and bitter,

> The Master still bore himself erect . . . perhaps with effort. . . .
> He had all the gravity and something of the splendour of Satan
> in the 'Paradise Lost'. I could not help but see the man with
> admiration, and was only surprised I saw him with so little fear.

> But indeed . . . it seemed as if his authority were quite
> vanished and his teeth all drawn. We had known him a magi-
> cian that controlled the elements; and here he was, trans-
> formed into an ordinary gentleman, chatting like his neigh-
> bours at the breakfast board. . . .[18]

James now wants enough of a reasonable settlement to go his
own way, and it is now Henry who denies this and leaves him in the
intolerable position of having to answer to Mackellar for bed and
board. It is outstanding how James now adapts himself through a
saving sardonicism to his demeaning role. He almost – and deliberately – parodies himself in his relation with Mackellar, as he draws
himself up in anger in the halls of his ancestors when Mackellar
tells him that he has only to keep in with him for his needs to be
supplied, then deliberately deflates the situation by wryly commenting that this is a pleasing return to the principles of childhood.
He, not Mackellar, creates that peculiarly intimate love-hate tolerance between them, and he tries on the *Nonesuch* to explain in
metaphor to Mackellar what the difference is between their values
and what may be the reality of Henry's attitude towards him. Just as
Hogg's *Justified Sinner* summed itself up in the Auchtermuchty
folk tale, so James crystallises his case in the tale of the Count and
the Baron. Briefly and allegorically the tale told of long-standing
enmity between the two. The ground does not matter, says James;
but in the most subtle way possible the Count brings about the
Baron's destruction, without blame attaching to himself in any
way. This story goes to the heart of the novel. Reading it for the
moment in the light of an interpretation sympathetic to James, we
are reminded that throughout the novel James has continuously
made use of the bible story of Jacob and Esau, with Henry always
cast in the role of deceiving Jacob. Is he now trying to tell Mackellar
that Henry is far more devious than Mackellar could ever realise?
That he, James, has suffered from a subtlety beyond his own? I
submit that the very lack of identification of either Henry or James
with Count or Baron allows this possibility; and further, that the
sequel, Mackellar's murder attempt and James's responses to it,
take us as close as we are allowed to the essence of James. James
tries to explain himself to Mackellar.

> 'Life is a singular thing. . . . You suppose yourself to love my
> brother. I assure you, it is merely custom. . . . Had you instead
> fallen in with me, you would today be as strong upon my side.'

Mackellar has no time for this attempt, and typically casts his
description of it in reductive and prejudicial terms.

> But he was now fairly started in his new course of justification, with which he wearied me throughout the remainder of the passage. . . . 'But now that I know you are a human being,' he would say, 'I can take the trouble to explain myself. For I assure you I am human too, and have my virtues, like my neighbours.'[19]

And James realises that Mackellar will once more return to his former prejudices when he is again with Henry.

In all their exchanges, there gradually develops a sense that we are observing diametrically opposed human types; types that are related to Stevenson's ideas of 'Providence' and 'Chance'. I suggest that Mackellar, however black or white we read him, speaks for Stevenson of that world of conventional and revealed religious orthodoxy. He becomes Stevenson's most subtle expression of his mingled feelings for pious respectability, family solidarity, Bible-based moral values; and conversely, that James, however we decide on his lack or possession of residual morality, represents a move by Stevenson towards a modern world of disillusion, scepticism, lack of faith in benevolent determinism. Thus James relies on Chance to decide his destiny, and thus he is compelled to be the outsider, the stoic rebel, the causeless hero. Their plight, that of traditional Scottish Conservatism locked in misunderstanding with rootless Disbelief, is summed up in a telling exchange as they leave Durrisdeer.

> 'Ah, Mackellar,' said he, 'do you think I have never a regret?'
>
> 'I do not think you could be so bad a man,' said I, 'if you had not all the machinery to be a good one.'
>
> 'No, not all,' says he: 'not all. You are there in error. The malady of not wanting, my evangelist.'[20]

I now leave my two interpretations; or rather, back off from them to look at the significance of their sitting beside one another in uneasy relation.

My final claim for this novel is that it is the finest expression of what Stevenson, like Hogg, Scott, Douglas Brown, MacDougall Hay, and even later writers like Gibbon, exemplified in their own crises of identity, and what they successfully managed to objectify into fictional vision. The Durrisdeer family and estate represents the estate of Scotland, like Gibbon's Kinraddie in *Sunset Song* or Brown's Barbie. Their history, going back to Thomas of Ercildoune's prophecy that there would be an ill day for them when one tied and one rode (Henry tied and James rode), back to the Reformation, and back to the wise old Lord that we meet as existing

Master, can be taken as eponymous, and symbolic of deleterious change in the nature of Scotland. The fragmenting effect of the Jacobite Rebellion ruins the integrity of the wise Master; and, leaving as he does such opposite and dissociated types as Henry and James, mirror images of each other and inheritors each of only a part of his wholeness, he himself becomes both literally and figuratively an anachronism in the novel, destroyed by the family division into Head and Heart. Henry and Mackellar are of course those forces of sober and arid Head; account-watching, love-repelling, feeling-repressing. James and Burke are their polar twins: romantic, self-indulgent, adept in the manipulation of feeling to the point of irresponsibility. 'Gnatique, patrisque, alma, precor, miserere', says the old Lord on his death bed; and he is weeping for the two sons, the hostile children of a divided country, who have as their badge the stained glass window bearing the family crest which Mackellar notices has an empty, clear lozenge of glass at its heart where their quarrel took the heart out of their identity, when the coin was flung through the window.

What makes this novel superior to others that have employed the same symbolic opposition is the way it rises above taking sides. Neither of these forces, brothers, opposing sets of qualities, have Right as their monopoly. The devil metaphor here, as opposed to Scott's usage, is flexible and destructive of either claim to rightness. The brothers thus rightly and symbolically share the same grave, having symbolically exiled themselves from their native and interior land.

Thus, briefly, but I hope effectively, I now justify the changing narrators, and the changing locations. If the meaning of the novel is in polarisation of values and human qualities, then the telling and location of the novel echoes that polarisation. Mackellar tells us much in his dry, domestic manner; but the manner of Burke, his chevalier style, reminds us that Mackellar too has his opposite, in its excessively flowery, self-indulgent *apologia* for the *picaresque*. Similarly, and echoing the theme of the brotherly opposition, there are domestic scenes and exotically placed foreign scenes. There is Henry's landscape of grey buildings and rain, and there is James's landscape of pirate deck and swamp. What is important is the final movement to a frozen wilderness, which worried Stevenson but does not at all worry the reader who has seen his instinctive skill in displacing both brothers from their humdrum or exotic backgrounds. If the results of history upon Scottish psyche were not just polarisation, but repression within each polarised part of its opposite, then the parts destroy each other with an unrealised and sterile longing for each other. This was Hogg's 'love-hate' relationship of Sinner and Devil; but for Stevenson the psychological fragmentation was even more complex, and more thoroughly tragic. Thus his brothers share the same grave, with balanced inscriptions which reflect the no-man's-land between them.

Stevenson thus rose above his own personal divisions on this one occasion, transforming what, on the whole, was a confused and immature vision into a remarkably modern and widely applicable comment on the difficulty of arriving in a Godless age at moral conclusion. He thus objectifies his own troubled mind, his relations with family and Scotland, the relations of any creative and troubled mind with Scotland as a whole, and a kind of spiritual fragmentation which is universal. There is Mackellar and James in many of us, Scots or not; and their goodness or otherwise is almost impossible to ascertain. I am left always, after reading the *Master*, with one of Stevenson's exotic descriptions of a physically arresting situation which symbolically says so much more; in this case, the scene where, on the *Nonesuch*, Mackellar, fascinated as a bird by a snake, watches the Master change position, endlessly.

> It was here we were sitting: our feet hanging down, the Master betwixt me and the side, and I holding on with both hands to the grating of the cabin skylight; for it struck me it was a dangerous position, the more so as I had before my eyes a measure of our evolutions in the person of the Master, which stood out in the break of the bulwarks against the sun. Now his head would be in the zenith and his shadow fall quite beyond the *Nonesuch* on the further side; and now he would swing down till he was underneath my feet, and the line of the sea leaped high above him like the ceiling of a room.[21]

If Mackellar had thought, he would have realised that he too was changing perspective for the Master, albeit his head was not in sunlight. I suppose, in the end, that what makes James more attractive, if not morally superior, to Mackellar or Henry, is that he has perspectives which Stevenson managed finally to give him, which we share, and which are denied to the Ephraim Mackellars or Henry Ballantraes.

References
1   E. M. Forster, *Aspects of the Novel* (London 1962: Pelican Edition) 45.
2   R. L. Stevenson, *Weir of Hermiston* (Chatto and Windus 1922) 112.

3 Francis Hart, *The Scottish Novel: a Critical Survey* (London 1978) 114-30.

4 R. L. Stevenson, *Kidnapped* and *Catriona* (Collins) 411-12.

5 Angus Macdonald, 'Modern Scots Novelists', in *Edinburgh Essays on Scots Literature* (Edinburgh 1933).

6 George Kitchin, 'John Galt', ibid., 113.

7 Coleman O. Parsons, *Witchcraft and Demonology in Scott's Fiction* (Edinburgh and London 1964) 296.

8 Edwin Muir, *Scott and Scotland; the Predicament of the Scottish Writer* (London 1936) *passim* and p.115.

9 John Speirs, *The Scots Literary Tradition* (London 1962) 142-51.

10 Edwin Muir, *Latitudes* (London, n.d.) 31-47.

11 Edwin Eigner, *Robert Louis Stevenson and Romantic Tradition* (Princeton 1966).

12 ibid., 212-13.

13 Alastair Fowler, 'Parables of Adventure: the debateable novels of Robert Louis Stevenson' in *Nineteenth-Century Scottish Fiction*, ed. Ian Campbell (Manchester 1979) 105.

14 Robert Louis Stevenson, *The Master of Ballantrae* and *Weir of Hermiston* (Everyman, 55) '. . . but I have never had much toleration for the female sex, possibly not much understanding; and . . . I have even shunned their company. Not only do I see no cause to regret this diffidence in myself, but have invariably remarked that most unhappy consequences follow those who were less wise.'

15 ibid., 2.

16 ibid., 78.

17 ibid., 79.

18 ibid., 117.

19 ibid., 140-1.

20 ibid., 129.

21 ibid., 135.

On Kidnapped

Kidnapped is like *Treasure Island* in some ways and unlike it in others. To start with the likenesses. 1) Both of them are among those works – *Dr Jekyll and Mr Hyde* and *A Child's Garden of Verses* are others – which have suffered nothing from the disparagement or neglect by the critics of Stevenson's work in general. The common reader has taken them to his heart. 2) Both *Kidnapped* and *Treasure Island* are good boys' books. By that I do not mean that they are books for good boys. Nor do I wish to be taken as endorsing the tiresome and anti-literary custom of sorting out books on the basis of their supposed suitability to particular 'age-groups'. Literature is not like that. But authors' intentions – while not necessarily decisive for criticism – have to be taken into account, and there is no doubt that authors have intended to write such things. I would define a good boys' book as a book which the author meant to be a boys' book and which does in fact appeal to many boys. (It is not necessarily a book which adults think boys like ; still less one they think boys ought to like.) Both *Kidnapped* and *Treasure Island* clearly satisfy that definition, and as far as *Kidnapped* is concerned Stevenson seems to have indicated his intention, at any rate as it was at the moment of completing the book, by calling it *Kidnapped* and publishing it in *Young Folks*. 3) *Kidnapped* is like *Treasure Island* in having obvious 'boys' book' qualities. Both have a youthful hero, who has exciting adventures. Neither has what film producers used to call a love interest – for the people who use that term would not apply it to David's relations with Alan, or the author's passion for the countryside round Edinburgh. What is meant is that neither book has a heroine. The only important female character in *Kidnapped* is the fine lassie who helps David and Alan to cross the Forth. For a love interest in the Hollywood sense we have to wait for the sequel, *Catriona*. 4) Both *Kidnapped*

and *Treasure Island,* though in varying degrees, convey signals to
the reader that he is being invited to join the author in a game. As
Henry James, best of Stevenson's critics, puts it: 'What he prizes
most in the boy's ideal is the imaginative side of it, the capacity for
successful make-believe.'[1] No author has surpassed Stevenson in
his power to recover this part of the secret joys and private poetry of
childhood and youth. Remember his fable of 'The Lantern-Bear-
ers'. He pictures a camp of small urchins who carry their smelly tin
lanterns buttoned under their overcoats. He thinks how silly they
must seem to an onlooker who does not understand their rapture,
sheltering in the cold sand on a bleak sea-shore on a dark autumn
night. 'To miss the joy,' he says, 'is to miss all. . . . Hence the
haunting and truly spectral unreality of realistic books. Hence,
when we read the English realists, the incredulous wonder with
which we observe the hero's constancy under the submerging tide
of dulness, and how he bears up with his jibbing sweetheart, and
endures the chatter of idiot girls, and stands by his whole un-
featured wilderness of an existence. . . . Hence in the French, in
that meat-market of middle-aged sensuality, the disgusted surprise
with which we see the hero drift side-long, and practically quite
untempted, into every description of misconduct and dishonour.
In each, we miss the personal poetry, the enchanted atmosphere,
that rainbow of fancy that clothes what is naked and seems to
ennoble what is base; in each, life falls dead like dough, instead of
soaring away like a balloon into the colours of the sunset; each is
true, each inconceivable; for no man lives in the external truth,
among salts and acids, but in the warm, phantasmagoric chamber of
his brains, with the painted windows and the storied walls.'[2]
5) Both *Kidnapped* and *Treasure Island* share to a superlative
degree a quality without which few books are popular, something
that looks so easy that we tend to take it for granted, and yet it is as
rare as all good things are. Johnson says in *The Rambler* (no. 122):
'Of the various kinds of speaking and writing, which serve neces-
sity or promote pleasure, none appears so artless or easy as simple
narration; for what should make him that knows the whole order
and progress of an affair unable to relate it? Yet we hourly find such
an endeavour to entertain or instruct us by recitals, clouding the
facts which they intend to illustrate, and losing themselves and
their auditors in the wilds of digression, or the mazes of con-
fusion.'[3] Corresponding to this narrative fluency we have in Stevenson, what does not always go with it, the power to make a clear-cut
plot-outline. Stevenson himself sets forth the outline of *Kidnapped*

in his sub-title: 'being the adventures of David Balfour; how he
was kidnapped and cast away; his sufferings in a desert isle; his
journey in the West Highlands; his acquaintance with Alan Breck
Stewart and other notorious Highland Jacobites; with all that he
suffered at the hands of his uncle, Ebenezer Balfour of Shaws, falsely so-called: written by himself, and now set forth by Robert Louis
Stevenson.' Well, that *is* what *Kidnapped* is about. But imagine
having to write an equivalent summary of *The Way We Live Now*,
or *Little Dorrit*! 6) Finally, both *Kidnapped* and *Treasure Island*
offer many satisfactions to the reader who is not only interested in
what is said, but also in how it is said. The boy who likes *Kidnapped* better than some ordinary adventure tale is not interested in
'style'; but perhaps he intuitively appreciates that his preference for
Kidnapped lies in Stevenson's superior ability to make the things
happen that we are to understand to have happened. And once he
has become conscious of that, he has learned what 'style' means.

> About half way down, the wind sprang up in a clap and shook
> the tower, and died again; the rain followed; and before I had
> reached the ground level it fell in buckets. I put out my head
> into the storm, and looked along towards the kitchen. The
> door, which I had shut behind me when I left, now stood open,
> and shed a little glimmer of light; and I thought I could see a
> figure standing in the rain, quite still, like a man hearkening.
> And then there came a blinding flash, which showed me my
> uncle plainly, just where I had fancied him to stand; and hard
> upon the heels of it, a great tow-row of thunder.
>   (ch. 4)

> It came all of a sudden when it did, with a rush of feet and a
> roar, and then a shout from Alan, and a sound of blows and
> someone crying out as if hurt. I looked back over my shoulder,
> and saw Mr Shuan in the doorway, crossing blades with Alan.
>   'That's him that killed the boy!' I cried.
>   'Look to your window!' said Alan; and as I turned back to my
> place, I saw him pass his sword through the mate's body.
>   (ch. 10)

> The mountains on either side were high, rough and barren,
> very black and gloomy in the shadow of the clouds, but all
> silver-laced with little watercourses where the sun shone upon
> them. It seemed a hard country, this of Appin, for people to
> care about as much as Alan did.
>   (ch. 17)

> . . . the sun shone upon a little moving clump of scarlet close in

along the waterside to the north. It was much of the same red as
soldier's coats; every now and then, too, there came little
sparks and lighnings, as though the sun had struck upon
bright steel.

(ch. 17)

Where are the frills and mannerisms of which Stevenson has been
so often accused? '"Look to your window!" said Alan; and as I
turned back to my place, I saw him pass his sword through the
mate's body.' If we are to talk about literary influences at all, it is the
plain style of Defoe that comes to mind. But it is the plain style of
Defoe handled by a sensuous artist. The same could be said of
Treasure Island.

So much for the likenesses between the two books. Now for the
unlikenesses. First, *Kidnapped* is a real travel book. The topography is carefully worked out. You can follow the actual route of
David and Alan (which Frank Morley does in his *Literary Britain*),
either literally, or on a map – preferably an eighteenth-century map
– as you can trace the whole Scottish journey of Johnson and
Boswell, twenty-two years after. Morley sets it out in all the detail
Stevenson carefully provided; how the brig *Covenant*, bearing
Alan Breck and David Balfour, having cleared Iona, struck and was
lost on the Torran rocks (Stevenson, it seems, puts them closer to
Mull than the map shows); so that they were castaways in a land of
Alan's hereditary foes, the Campbells. From then on the route of
the travellers may be traced from Glen Coe eastward across the
Rannoch Moor, south from Ben Alder to the Braes of Balquhidder –
Scott country, *The Lady of the Lake* and parts of *Rob Roy* – and so to
the final stage of the fugitives' journey, when Alan and David,
having bypassed Stirling, make their way along the north shore of
the Firth of Forth, which they are enabled to cross by the help of the
lass from whom they bought bread and cheese, and, landing near
Carriden, are in just the right place for the denouement at the
House of Shaws, placed by Stevenson in the countryside he knew
from his youth. For the parting with Alan, David walked with him
towards Edinburgh as far as the hill of Corstorphine, and there was
the halting-place bearing the same name as the halting-place Dr
Johnson had noticed at Glen Crose: Rest-and-be-thankful. It
marked Johnson's farewell to his Scottish peregrinations: and
what better end for an adventure story than Rest-and-be-thankful?

Kidnapped, then, unlike *Treasure Island*, is bound up with real
geography, and this element of reality is part of its essence. But
there is a deeper difference. *Treasure Island* may or may not have a

high place in literature (I myself would rank it very high) but no one could dispute its outstanding quality as a work of what is called genre fiction. It is a pirate story – surely the best pirate story ever written? But *Kidnapped* is less self-evident generically. Is it a travel book, or an adventure story, or a historical novel? It seems to be all these things, and yet not precisely any of them. The same sort of problem arises in the discussion of *Huckleberry Finn*, and it suggests that there are some occasions when the guidance we get from the concept of 'genre fiction' ceases to be helpful. Stevenson knew exactly what he was doing in *Treasure Island*. He was writing in the genre 'pirate story', but improving it. But what about *Kidnapped*? Stevenson wrote to Watts-Dunton that it was originally conceived as another *Treasure Island*, but when he saw how to use his historical material the novel developed in an unexpected direction. His interest in the Appin murder may well be the genetic explanation for the difference between the two books. But reference to these antecedents, to the author's original intentions, does not help us much to understand the meaning of *Kidnapped*. For, as Stevenson tells us, in this book and in this book only, 'the characters took the bit between their teeth; all at once they became detached from the flat paper, they turned their backs on me bodily; and from that time my task was stenographic; it was they who spoke, it was they who wrote the remainder of the story.' There are other famous examples of this kind of thing in the history of literature, and Stevenson's account of the writing of *Kidnapped* suggests that I have not begged the question in speaking of its 'meaning'. It has a meaning in a sense in which *St Ives*, for example, has not. *St Ives* is full of author's intentions, the formulae of romantic adventure, but critical examination suggests that in carrying them out the author's deeper imagination was not involved.

Stevenson does not tell us at what precise point the characters took the bit between their teeth. But the fact that this occurred at all suggests that it is the structure of *Kidnapped* that provides the clue to its interpretation. Let us look into the structure. *Kidnapped* obviously consists of two stories, David Balfour's and Alan Breck's. Their stories begin to interweave when in a night of thick weather the *Covenant* ran down a boat and Alan Breck leaped from the stern and clutched the brig's bowsprit. And their destinies become inseparably interwoven with the Appin murder. Clearly the murder of Red Colin is pivotal. It leads to complications which are not cleared up in *Kidnapped*, and had to wait some years till Stevenson wrote a sequel, *Catriona*. This feature of the book has been ad-

versely criticised. '*Kidnapped*,' says Ernest Baker, 'is only a con-
geries of events. . . . The Appin murder is only a mechanical centre,
not an organic motive ; . . . it has nothing to do with David or Alan.'[4]
So this critic finds *Kidnapped*, like *Catriona*, just a miscellany of
adventure, though admirably pieced together. And Baker thinks
this typical of Stevenson. 'He seems not to have visualized his
novels as complete wholes, but to have built them up from one
episode to the next.' 'Except *Treasure Island*, story rather than
novel, and *Weir of Hermiston*, Stevenson's masterpieces in fiction
are in the briefer and more concentrated genre.' Other critics (Frank
Swinnerton, for example) have concurred in finding that Stevenson's real gift was for the short story. Let us then look more closely
at the construction of *Kidnapped* and see whether analysis can
disclose an essential unifying theme.

The narrative seems to me to fall into five movements. Chapters 1
to 6 are concerned with David and his uncle ; this movement ends
with the kidnapping. Chapters 7 to 13 tell the story of David on
board the *Covenant*, and culminate with the loss of the brig. The
third movement, chapters 14 to the middle of 17, recounts David's
adventures without Alan. This movement is spectacularly cut short
by the Appin murder, which David witnesses. The fourth movement, from the middle of chapter 17 to the end of chapter 25, is
about David on the run with Alan : it includes the famous flight in
the heather. Chapter 26, the crossing of the Forth, may be seen as
something of an intermezzo, leading to the final movement, chapters 27 to 30, which tell of David's return to Shaws and the recovery
of his inheritance.

The first movement is full of conscious and affectionate references to the tradition of romance, ballad, folktale – genre-signals, so
to speak.

> . . . there came up into my mind (quite unbidden by me and
> even discouraged) a story like some ballad I had heard folks
> singing, of a poor lad that was a rightful heir and a wicked
> kinsman that tried to keep him from his own.
>   (ch. 4)

When David on the *Covenant* tells Riach his story, 'he declared it
was like a ballad.' This generic indication is given explicit literary
expression in the final movement, by the cultivated Rankeillor,
who humorously speculates on what kind of book David and he are
going to be in.

> This is a great epic, a great Odyssey of yours. You must tell it,
> sir, in a sound Latinity when your scholarship is riper ; or in

English if you please, though for my part I prefer the stronger tongue. You have rolled much; *quae regio in terris* – what parish in Scotland (to make a homely translation) has not been filled with your wanderings? You have shown, besides, a singular aptitude for getting into false positions; and yet, upon the whole, for behaving well in them.

(ch. 27)

This generic reference is rounded off by David himself in chapter 29. 'So the beggar in the ballad had come home; and when I lay down that night on the kitchen chests, I was a man of means and had a name in the country.'

This way of looking at *Kidnapped* seems to offer the only explanation of the otherwise inexplicable incident of Jennet Clouston. She is introduced with strong emphasis, as a Meg Merrilies figure calling down doom on Uncle Ebenezer and the House of Shaws: '. . . tell him this makes the twelve hunner and nineteen time that Jennet Clouston has called down the curse on him and his house, byre and stable, man, guests, and master, wife, miss, or bairn – black, black, be their fall!' (ch. 2). She is mentioned again in chapter 6, when the landlord of the Hawes Inn says of Ebenezer: 'He's a wicked auld man, and there's many would like to see him girning in a tow [rope]; Jennet Clouston and mony mair that he had harried out of house and hame . . .' ringing it out like a Scots alliterative poem. But after that we hear no more of Jennet Clouston. Why is this? Stevenson, a master of narrative if ever there was one, must have known that to introduce so colourful a character, with so strong an emphasis, must leave the reader in pleasurable suspense. But he never resolves it. The only common-sense, 'external' explanation I can think of is that Stevenson changed his design. But if this explanation is rejected as unverifiable, the alternative must be that Jennet Clouston is a genre-signal: a sort of musical quotation from the old kind of romance.

It might be said that Uncle Ebenezer himself belongs entirely to that world. I wish I had time to look at the different facets of Uncle Ebenezer, that 'man of principles' as he calls himself, the most disagreeable figure in Stevenson's gallery of bad Lowlanders. (He is not, indeed, totally unsympathetic, but then no one in Stevenson is totally unsympathetic.) His introduction is masterly.

I was in two minds whether to run away; but anger got the upper hand, and I began instead to rain kicks and buffets on the door, and to shout aloud for Mr. Balfour. I was in full career, when I heard the cough right overhead, and jumping back and

looking up, beheld a man's head in a tall nightcap, and the bell
mouth of a blunderbuss at one of the first-storey windows.

'It's loaded,' said a voice.

(ch. 2)

David's introduction to him reminds me a little of Becky Sharp's
introduction to Sir Pitt Crawley in *Vanity Fair*. Edwin M. Eigner,
perhaps more to the point, has recalled Lockwood's reception at
Wuthering Heights. At any rate, it is storybook stuff. Even the
dismayed David, as well as the reader, finds a kind of artistic
pleasure in contemplating Ebenezer.

> He fetched another cup from the shelf; and then, to my great
> surprise, instead of drawing more beer, he poured an accurate
> half from one cup to the other. There was a kind of nobleness
> in this that took my breath away; if my uncle was certainly a
> miser, he was one of that thorough breed that goes near to
> make the vice respectable.

Henry James, however, was a little unhappy about him: 'The cruel
and miserly uncle . . . is rather in the tone of superseded tradition,
and the tricks he plays upon his ingenuous nephew are a little like
those of country conjurers; in these pages we feel that Mr Stevenson is thinking too much of what a "boys' paper" is expected to
contain.' Perhaps so; but to connoisseurs of that tradition the first
movement of *Kidnapped* offers superb examples of the revitalizing
of its formulae. One of its characteristic devices is what Aristotle
calls the *anagnorisis*, or moment of recognition; there is no better
example of it in literature than what happened on the stair at Shaws.

> . . . as I advanced, it seemed to me the stair grew airier and a
> thought more lightsome; and I was wondering what might be
> the cause of this change, when a second blink of the summer
> lightning came and went. If I did not cry out, it was because
> fear had me by the throat; and if I did not fall, it was more by
> Heaven's mercy than by my own strength. It was not only that
> the flash shone in on every side through breaches in the wall,
> so that I seemed to be clambering aloft upon an open scaffold,
> but the same passing brightness showed me the steps were of
> unequal length, and that one of my feet rested that moment
> within two inches of the well.

(ch. 4)

Another 'recognition' device is the use of the pre-story, the
explanation in the final movement of how Uncle Ebenezer came to
be what he was. There is again some likeness to *Wuthering Heights*,
when Rankeillor explains:

'. . . the matter hinges on a love affair.'

'Truly,' said I, 'I cannot well join that notion with my uncle.'

'But your uncle, Mr. David, was not always ugly. He had a fine, gallant air . . .'

'It sounds like a dream,' said I.

'Ay, ay,' said the lawyer, 'that is how it is with youth and age.'

. . .

'. . . The one man took the lady, the other the estate.'

'. . . this piece of Quixotry on your father's part, as it was unjust in itself, has brough forth a monstrous family of injustices.'

(ch. 28)

Stevenson was to make this kind of story the centre of interest in *The Master of Ballantrae*. But here it must be judged, in Jamesian language, to belong to the treatment rather than the essence of the story : it is another genre-signal.

Once David is on board the *Covenant* Henry James has no further objections – until the end of the book ; 'The remaining five-sixths . . . deserve to stand by *Henry Esmond,* as a fictive autobiography in archaic form.'[5] Yet the second movement of *Kidnapped* can be still seen as conforming to Stevenson's theory of romance. This can be summarised as the placing of an unromantic hero in a romantic situation, and so as the opposite of some of the great works of realist fiction : *Madame Bovary,* for example, is the tragedy of a romantic person in an unromantic situation. We may see also in *Kidnapped* other features of Stevensonian romance : the comparative 'transparency' of the hero ; the absence of the omniscient author (and hence of psychological analysis of the characters) ; the stress on striking incident. We note the kinship with folktales and fairytales which John Buchan saw in the great Victorian novelists : the 'good story' ; the characters recognisable as 'real types' ; the method of reproducing reality not as an inventory of details, but by 'judicious selection' ; the story-teller's primary interest in the events he has to tell of, and not in his own reactions to them : he does not obtrude his moods.[6]

But Buchan lays equal emphasis on another aspect of this tradition : the moral aspect. The story-teller passes moral judgments on his characters ; he regards some as definitely good and some as definitely bad. And finally 'he has a dominant purpose, a lesson, if you like, to teach, a creed to suggest'. This brings us to the question

of the morality, the *ethos*, of Stevensonian romance. To discuss this
is to go to the heart of *Kidnapped*. It is surprising that F.R. Leavis
excluded Stevenson from his 'Great Tradition'. Leavis seems to
require from a great novelist a profound concern with moral problems. But was there ever an author more concerned with moral
problems than Stevenson? – not to speak of theological problems?
We are never far away from the Scottish Catechism in Stevenson,
with its awe-inspiring first question: 'What is the whole duty of
man?'

But perhaps Leavis would not have found Stevenson's treatment
of moral problems profound enough. Now certainly the morality of
romance is simple. It belongs to what Gilbert Ryle, in his essay on
Jane Austen, calls the 'Calvinist', as opposed to the 'Aristotelian',
pattern. 'In the eighteenth century, and in other centuries too,
moralists tended to belong to one of two camps . . . the Calvinist
camp . . . thinks, like a criminal lawyer, of human beings as . . .
Saved or Damned, Elect or Reject, children of Virtue or children of
Vice, heading for Heaven or heading for Hell, White or Black,
Innocent or Guilty, Saints or Sinners . . . The Calvinist's moral
psychology is correspondingly bi-polar. People are dragged up-
wards by Soul or Spirit or Reason or Conscience; but they are
dragged down by Body or Flesh or Passion or Pleasure or Inclina-
tion. A man is an unhappy combination of a white angelic part and a
black satanic part. At the best, the angelic part has the satanic part
cowed and starved and subjugated now, and can hope to be released
altogether from it in the future. Man's life here is either a life of Sin
or it is a life of self-extrication from Sin . . . the seducer in *The
Vicar of Wakefield* . . . is wickedness incarnate . . . [like] Fanny
Burney's bad characters. Johnson in *The Rambler* . . . persons who
are all black . . . no Tuesday morning attributes.'[7]

In contrast is the Aristotelian pattern of ethical ideas. 'People
differ from each other in degree and not in kind, not in respect just
of a single generic Sunday attribute, but a whole spectrum of
specific weekday attributes. . . . A is a bit more irritable and
ambitious than B, less indolent and less sentimental. C is meaner
and quicker-witted than D, and D is greedier and more athletic than
C. A person is not black and white, but iridescent with all the
colours of the rainbow . . . not a flat plane, but a highly irregular
solid . . . better than most in one respect, about level with the
average in another respect, and a bit, perhaps a big bit, deficient in a
third respect. In fact he is like people we really know, in a way in
which we do not know and could not know any people who are just

Bad or else just Good.' Ryle's argument is that Jane Austen's moral ideas are, with certain exceptions, ideas of the Aristotelian and not of the Calvinist pattern. 'Much as she had learned from Johnson, this she had not learned from him.'

How then is Stevenson's morality, in his fiction, to be classified – Calvinist or Aristotelian? On the face of it, it is Calvinist. There is no doubt that Uncle Ebenezer is Bad. What about the captain and crew of the *Covenant*? They are mixed. But they are seen as black-and-white mixtures, not 'iridescent'. The poor crazy boy Ransome thinks Captain Hoseason wholly bad, but David discovers that 'he was neither so good as I supposed him, nor quite so bad as Ransome did; for, in fact, he was two men, and left the better one behind as soon as he set foot on board his vessel.' He is, in fact, a case of Jekyll and Hyde, not in the subtle sense that Stevenson had in mind in that story, but in the popular interpretation of it. He is a cold-blooded villain – literally:

> 'Captain Hoseason,' returned my uncle, 'you keep your room unco hot.'
>
> 'It's a habit I have, Mr. Balfour,' said the skipper. 'I'm a cold-rife man in my nature; I have a cold blood, sir. There's neither fur nor flannel – no, sir, nor hot rum will warm up what they call the temperature. Sir, it's the same with most men that have been carbonadoed, as they call it, in the south seas.'
>
> 'Well, well,' replied my uncle, 'we must all be in the way we're made.'
>
> (ch. 6)

Yet, he says, 'I am true-blue Protestant, and I thank God for it.' 'It was,' says David, 'the first word of any religion I had ever heard from him, but I learnt afterwards that he was a great church-goer while on shore.' He loves his mother.

> I heard a gun fire, and supposed the storm had proved too strong for us, and we were firing signals of distress. . . . Yet it was no such matter; but (as I was afterwards told) a common habit of the captain's. . . . We were then passing, it appeared, within some miles of Dysart, where the brig was built, and where old Mrs. Hoseason, the captain's mother, had come some years before to live; and whether outward or inward bound, the *Covenant* was never suffered to go by that place by day, without a gun fired and colours shown.
>
> (ch. 7)

David learns to see similar dualities in the crew of the *Covenant*.

> . . . I found there was a strange peculiarity about our two

mates : that Mr. Riach was sullen, unkind, and harsh when he
was sober, and Mr. Shuan would not hurt a fly except when he
was drinking. I asked about the captain; but I was told drink
made no difference upon that man of iron.

   (ch. 7)

David has to learn that human nature is strangely mixed. But there
is no doubt about the ingredients of the mixture : good and evil. We
have terrifying glimpses of pure evil.

   . . . two seamen appeared in the scuttle, carrying Ransome in
   their arms; and the ship at that moment giving a great sheer
   into the sea, and the lantern swinging, the light fell direct on
   the boy's face. It was as white as wax, and had a look upon it
   like a dreadful smile.
   . . .
   'Sit down !' roars the captain. 'Ye sot and swine, do ye know
   what ye've done? Ye've murdered the boy !'
   Mr. Shuan seemed to understand; for he sat down again, and
   put up his hand to his brow.
   'Well,' he said, 'he brought me a dirty pannikin !'

   (ch. 8)

What makes it so terrible is what Hannah Arendt calls the banality
of evil: appalling crimes are committed by ordinary, helpless human beings.

   . . . Hoseason walked up to his chief officer, took him by the
   shoulder, led him across to his bunk, and bade him lie down
   and go to sleep, as you might speak to a bad child. The murderer cried a little, but he took off his sea-boots and obeyed.

   (ch. 8)

'You may think it strange,' says David, 'but for all the horror I had, I
was still sorry for him. He was a married man, with a wife in Leith;
but whether or no he had a family, I have now forgotten; I hope
not.' In this second movement, then, we are still in a 'Calvinist'
moral world. It culminates in the defeat of the bad characters in the
fight in the roundhouse, and the loss of the brig.

   The third movement, when David and Alan are parted, shows
in comparison a slackening of intensity. Here, if anywhere, *Kidnapped* is open to the charge of being merely episodic. The incidents in this part of the book seem mainly designed to show the
disturbed state of the Highlands in the 1750s. But they may also be
put in deliberately to relieve tension. The comic note is prominent.
David's 'marooning' on Earraid is due, not to a malign fate, but to
his own folly and ignorance, as he himself ruefully recognises. Mr

Henderland is introduced to sound the note of positive goodness
and to remind us of David's piety. But he is also a semi-comic
character, with his roundabout way of gratifying his passion for
snuff while having ascetically renounced it. In short, the novel
becomes rather *picaresque* thereabouts, and some of the incidents
show a lack of inspiration. It has often been remarked that the
sinister blind catechist is much inferior, in thrilling suggestive-
ness, to blind Pew in *Treasure Island*.

The tension mounts again with the Appin murder. It is interesting to contrast this with the murder of Ransome..

> . . . just as he turned there came the shot of a firelock from
> higher up the hill; and with the very sound of it Glenure fell
> upon the road.
>
> 'O, I am dead!' he cried, several times over.
>
> The lawyer had caught him up and held him in his arms, the
> servant standing over and clasping his hands.
>
> (ch. 17)

The effect is quite different. The murder of Red Colin happens so
suddenly. We have not yet learned to care about him as we care
about Ransome. And it is a different kind of murder: a political
assassination, not an act of drunken cruelty. For David, however –
and this is the important point – there is no difference, morally
speaking. Murder is murder.

Morally speaking – but not psychologically. For this murder
David, because of his love for Alan, is involved in. He experiences
'a new kind of terror'.

> . . . It is one thing to stand the danger of your life, and quite
> another to run the peril of both life and character. The thing,
> besides, had come so suddenly, like thunder out of a clear sky,
> that I was all amazed and helpless.
>
> (ch. 17)

This, then, is the psychological turning-point of *Kidnapped*. We
pass from the timeless world of folktale, with its appropriate black-
and-white morality, to a historical world, with a problematic, relative, regionally and culturally conditioned morality. Aristotle pre-
sides, not Calvin. With the coming together again of David and
Alan both the genre and the ethos of *Kidnapped* have changed.
Generically, it becomes a pursuit story – and one with a historical
background.

The Appin murder is something that really happened. I am not
concerned here with who really was the murderer. (It seems, as a
matter of fact, that there was a conspiracy of the gentry of Appin.) I

am only concerned with the murder as Stevenson presents it. And one thing he is clear about: Alan was not the murderer. He is prepared to swear this, to David, on his holy dirk. David accepts it, and so must we. But this does not bridge the moral chasm between David and Alan. Alan does not think the killing of a Campbell is wrong. And he equivocates about his knowledge of the murderer's identity. What does a Campbell matter? There are plenty of others. The Campbells will take their revenge by the judicial murder of a Stewart. And Alan does not think they would be wrong to do that. The Duke of Argyll, the head of the clan, knows that if circumstances were reversed, a Stewart would do the same thing to a Campbell. In short, Alan recognises only a tribal morality. He gives voice naively to what Prestongrange in *Catriona* is to defend with all his formidable and sophisticated intellectual resources. His morals, says David helplessly, are 'tail-first'.

This is the beginning of David's moral ordeal. Hitherto his ordeal had been mainly physical. And it is to go on being physical: we are never allowed to forget that David, hero of romance as he may be, is constantly fainting because of his bad feet. And there is no more sustained evocation of a physical ordeal in literature than the flight in the heather: Stevenson was justly proud of it, arguing against Henry James that something an author has not in fact lived through can be more imaginatively stimulating than something he has lived through. But from now on it is to be a moral and psychological ordeal as well. First, the moral ordeal. The law, in *Kidnapped*, as in much imaginative literature, is the symbol of civilisation, order, the good. But what happens to a country in a time of troubles, when the law can be all too plausibly seen as an instrument of oppression of one faction by another? You cannot expect people who are persecuted by the law to respect it. But what happens is not that a better law replaces it, but that clan loyalty becomes all in all – or even more self-centred ideologies: it is clear that much of Alan Breck's 'code' consists of little more than personal vanity.

The general political and social implications of this lawlessness are explored more fully in *Catriona.* In *Kidnapped* the focus is more individual. The moral interest centres on the relationship between a civilised man and a primitive – as does the most memorable part of *Huckleberry Finn*. Eigner points out that Stevenson read *Huckleberry Finn* in 1885, and it was at this time that he dropped his plans for a highwayman novel and wrote *Kidnapped* instead. And many suggestive parallels can be drawn between

Stevenson and Mark Twain, notably the 'eternal boy' theme which
has figured so much in the criticism of both of them. But whether
or not Stevenson was influenced by *Huckleberry Finn*, David is like
Huck with Nigger Jim in having to undergo a conflict of impera-
tives. He is caught between his love for Alan and his reprobation of
Alan's morality. It is another case of what Leslie Fiedler has called
the theme of the Beloved Scoundrel, adumbrated in the relation of
Jim Hawkins to John Silver in *Treasure Island*: the moral ambiguity that results from a character's being both admired and condemned. (Was Achilles in the *Iliad* the first of these in literature?)
We must remember that – to use a distinction of Ronald Knox's –
David is a 'pathetic' rather than a 'drastic' character. On the whole,
things happen to him, while the Beloved Scoundrel is the one who
does things.

   The moral contrast between David and Alan has already appeared
in the second movement, in the fight in the roundhouse. David's
feelings are those of the civilised man.

> . . . what with the long suspense of the waiting, and the scurry
> and strain of our two spirits of fighting, and more than all, the
> horror I had of some of my own share in it, the thing was no
> sooner over than I was glad to stagger to a seat. There was that
> tightness of my chest that I could hardly breathe; the thought
> of the two men I had shot sat upon me like a nightmare.
>   (ch. 10)

Alan's reactions are those of the child, the primitive.

> Thereupon he turned to the four enemies, passed his sword
> clean through each of them, and tumbled them out of doors
> one after the other. As he did so, he kept humming, and
> singing, and whistling to himself, like a man trying to recall
> an air; only what *he* was trying was to make one. All the while,
> the flush was in his face, and his eyes were as bright as a
> five-year-old child's with a new toy. And presently he sat down
> upon the table, sword in hand; the air that he was making all
> the time began to run a little clearer, and then clearer still; and
> then out he burst with a great voice into a Gaelic song.
> . . .
> He came up to me with open arms. 'Come to my arms!' he
> cried, and embraced and kissed me hard upon both cheeks.
> 'David,' said he, 'I love you like a brother. And O, man,' he
> cried in a kind of ecstasy, 'am I no a bonny fighter?'
>   (ch. 10)

But at this stage there is no moral *problem*, because Alan is on the

side of good. In the central part of *Kidnapped* it is no longer clear
what is good or what is bad. Is Alan good or bad? Is he even a
mixture of good and bad? He is going to present St Peter with a
problem. Not that David ever gives up his 'Calvinist' moral views.
It is this above all that adds a special quality of pathos to the great
scene which is the climax of *Kidnapped*, the quarrel between David
and Alan. We have seen it coming, of course, from the beginning,
and the scene in which Alan gambles away David's money only
brings matters to a head. What follows has been justly praised by
Henry James for its psychological truth, its humour, and its pathos.

> . . . Alan had behaved like a child, and (what is worse) a
> treacherous child. . . .
>
> 'I will only say this to ye, David,' said Alan, very quietly,
> 'that I have long been owing ye my life, and now I owe ye
> money. Ye should try to make that burden light for me.'
> . . .
> He had just called me 'Whig'. I stopped.
>
> 'Mr Stewart . . . you are older than I am, and should know
> your manners. Do you think it either very wise or very witty to
> cast my politics in my teeth? I thought, where folk differed, it
> was the part of gentlemen to differ civilly; and if I did not, I
> may tell you I could find a better taunt than some of yours.'
> . . . he began to whistle a Jacobite air . . . made in mockery of
> General Cope's defeat at Prestonpans. . . . 'Why do ye take that
> air, Mr. Stewart? . . . Is that to remind me you have been beaten
> on both sides?'
> . . .
> . . . [Alan] drew his sword. But before I could touch his blade
> with mine, he had thrown it from him and fallen to the ground.
> 'Na, na,' he kept saying, 'na, na – I cannae, I cannae.'
> . . .
> 'Alan,' cried I, 'What makes ye so good to me? What makes ye
> care for such a thankless fellow?'
>
> 'Deed, and I don't know,' said Alan. 'For just precisely what
> I thought I liked about ye, was that ye never quarrelled; and
> now I like ye better!'
>   (ch. 24)

It is a fine example of one kind of love (what C. S. Lewis in his *Four
Loves* calls *philia*) rising for a moment to another, which he calls
agape. There is a little coda, both comic and touching, in which
Alan tries to stay at the level of 1 Corinthians and sacrifice his
vanity.

    . . . 'My poor man, will ye no be better on my back?'

    'Oh, Alan,' says I, 'and me a good twelve inches taller.'

    'Ye're no such a thing,' cried Alan with a start. 'There may be
a trifling matter of an inch or two; I'm no saying I'm just
exactly what ye would call a tall man, whatever; and I dare say,'
he added, his voice tailing off in a laughable manner, 'now
when I come to think of it, I dare say ye'll be just about right.
Ay, it'll be a foot, or near hand; or may be even mair!'

    (ch. 24)

Humour, imaginative insight, moral delicacy. But above all pathos:
what makes this episode especially pathetic is that the moral im-
passe between them, momentarily forgotten in this upsurge of
love, remains complete.

    It is notable how much emphasis there is in this part of *Kid-
napped* on the state of mind which David calls 'horror'. 'I was
conscious of no particular nightmare, only of a general, black,
abiding horror' (ch. 23). Of course David has been in a pretty
sullen, glowering frame of mind for most of *Kidnapped*: this is one
of the reasons why *Kidnapped* is 'a good boys' book'; that feeling
that the world is against you, that sulky rage against existence in
general, which filmed or dramatised versions of the book never
manage to convey. And of course David has plenty of dramatically
adequate reason for it, in what has happened to him: the boy reader
may enjoy David's adventures, but David himself did not. But I am
not sure that his ill-treatment and sufferings are entirely sufficient
to explain his mood. He has passed from being an innocent cast-
away to being a hunted criminal. He is on the wrong side: the
representative of civilisation is at odds with it. From being the
'good' romance-hero, he has become merely a member of a particular faction – a Lowland Whig, incongruously and fortuitously
thrown into the power of a Highland Jacobite.

    So it is that the fourth movement of *Kidnapped* develops many
paradoxes. We have already seen the child Alan contrasted with the
man David, yet in years David is the child and Alan the man. We
have seen, of course, the contrast of the Lowlander with the Highlander, and what may be called the Lowland view of things with the
Highland view of things. This contrast obviously has its basis in
history and observation. But Stevenson does not seem to be primarily concerned with it, as Scott was, in either historical or
picturesque terms. It is as if for him 'Lowland' and 'Highland'
stand for two possibilities of man, possibilities that might ideally
be realised in the same individual. And what David unwittingly

seems to register is that the individual who does not realise them both is lacking in something. I suspect that the true moral of *Dr Jekyll and Mr Hyde* is to be found here, not in the popular reading.

The essential story of *Kidnapped* could have been told as a beast-fable: the story of a wolf hunted by dogs. But to complicate matters many of the other wolves are on the side of the dogs, while the wolf is accompanied on his flight by a dog. Stevenson tells us in *Travels with a Donkey* that he feared dogs more than wolves. We might think of the contrast between Silver and the other pirates in *Treasure Island*: Silver is a 'dog', disciplined, self-controlled, prudent, who has gone to the bad. This, according to Stevenson, is the most dangerous kind of human being. The Lowland villain is more to be feared than the Highland villain; an ordered wickedness more to be feared than a wild wickedness. If, as Machiavelli says, the ideal ruler must combine the lion and the fox, we may say that for Stevenson the ideal man must combine the wolf and the dog – but only in their virtues.

With the crossing of the Forth we return to the key of romance. There is another fine example of a romance-device, what Aristotle calls the *peripeteia*, in David's defeat of his uncle. (Though it is noteworthy that even here the effective agent is Alan; David merely waits in the darkness, 'pathetic' rather than 'drastic' to the last.) The hero has come home from his ordeal with the savages, through which Alan has been his savage guide. Civilisation at last!

> . . . a very good house on the landward side, a house with beautiful clear glass windows, flowering knots upon the sills, the walls new-harled [newly rough-cast], and a chase-dog sitting yawning on the step like one that was at home.
>
> (ch. 27)

Yet the ending seems almost an anti-climax. This is what Henry James thought the other 'weak spot' in *Kidnapped*. He gave an external explanation for it: Stevenson's health. Stevenson was physically unable to complete more than one of the three stories he had started, so he wound up the story of David's inheritance, leaving the fate of Alan and James of the Glens undecided.

This may indeed have been the true state of affairs, and it accounts for the very subdued way *Kidnapped* ends. But it does not completely account for the *sadness* with which it ends. There is a similar sadness at the end of *Treasure Island*, but this sadness seems deeper. Jim's sadness can be explained as his realisation that the adventures are over (though I think there is more in it than that). But why does David feel 'something like remorse' at the end of *Kidnapped*? He is worried about Alan, of course, and James of the Glens. But their plight was not his fault. I think the use of the word 'remorse' suggests that we are here at the level of deep imagination. Without Silver, Jim is without something that he needs psychologically, but must reprobate morally. But that story is over. What is needed to complete *Kidnapped*? It might have been the beginning of a series, like *The Three Musketeers* of Stevenson's favourite Dumas (Alan may perhaps be inspired by D'Artagnan). He can have further adventures, because he is an adventurer: David is settled. Settled, but sad. How can there be a psychologically satisfying solution as far as David is concerned?

What is needed is some way in which to show concretely the ideal convergence of Highland and Lowland virtues. But it would be hard to follow this out in terms of the relation of David and Alan. They are not homosexuals. Whatever might have been the case in real life, their love in the book is that of *philia* only: *eros* plays no part. It could be, then, that in the sequel Catriona is a surrogate for Alan, and that Stevenson intended some symbolic significance in the marriage of David and Catriona, the union of Jacobite and Covenanter, the wild girl of Alban with the Westminster Confession. This might have a meaning in regard to the unity of sundered Scotland. It might have a more important meaning in the reconciliation of contrasting and conflicting impulses in the individual human soul.

However that may be, I do not think *Catriona* a complete artistic success. It contains some fine things. But Stevenson is only at his best in treating adult problems and pressures when he works behind the mask of a boy's story. Kipling may be a parallel here; and perhaps, again, Mark Twain. But, as Kipling would say, that is another story. *Kidnapped*, unlike *Catriona*, seems to me a complete and unified artistic success, and the sad ending is an essential part of it. Stevenson has not attempted to impose false unity on a dualism which haunted him to the end of his life.

References
1 'Robert Louis Stevenson, 1887', in Henry James,
   The House of Fiction, ed. Leon Edel (1957) 119.
2 'The Lantern Bearers', *The Works of Robert Louis
   Stevenson* (Edinburgh Edition 1894) vol. I, 353-5.
3 Samuel Johnson, *Works* (Yale edition 1969) vol. IV, 287.
4 E. Baker, *History of the English Novel* (1938) vol. IX, 315.
5 Henry James, op. cit., 136.
6 John Buchan, English Association pamphlet no.79.
7 Gilbert Ryle, *Collected Papers* (1971) vol. I, 284-5.

CHRISTOPHER HARVIE

The Politics of Stevenson

The astonishing reputation of Robert Louis Stevenson, for a couple of decades after his death, was based as much on his life – and not simply his efforts to transcend ill-health, but on the ironies of his circumstances – as on his actual output. That much is common-place. At the very least he became the literary monument enshrined in six successive editions of complete works (including much juvenilia, collaborative and incomplete work); on occasion he even went further than being a Sunday-school prize author and became a surrogate Apostle. His death of course helped. Avoiding bankrupt-cy and insanity, unlike Scott and Ruskin, he was seemingly struck down at the height of his powers, halfway through what was judged to be his greatest book, by what his own last written words called 'a wilful convulsion of brute nature'. To this the response of literary Britain was, as we know, spectacular, and subsequent controversy only enhanced it, yet detached critical assessment, which has grant-ed Stevenson a respectable place as a writer, was almost a half century in coming. Stevenson was a phenomenon, and spawned the sort of literature we associate with phenomena, like science fiction. How do we explain it?

Further, Stevenson was distanced from the great Victorian tradi-tion of high-minded social analysis, and even remarkably ignorant of it. We know he gave up on Carlyle, but if we search the main biographies for reference to Matthew Arnold, George Eliot, John Ruskin and their influence, we search in vain. Kipling, Wilde, Shaw and Yeats, who shared some of Stevenson's 'phenomenon' quality, were in some respects within this tradition, Stevenson was an outsider. Like them he made his entry during a critical period in taste and organisation, but his popularity remained a much more specifically literary one.

Stevenson's popularity came at a time of rapid change. The

tyranny of the circulating libraries was slackening, the old 'Three-decker' novel was on its way out. By the 1890s a new establishment would have arisen, in which authors were commercial proposi-tions, nurtured by agents, boosted into 'personalities' by articles in new and influential publications like Robertson Nicoll's *The Book-man* (1891), and rapidly produced in very cheap editions.[1] Although much of his success owed to the liberties Stevenson was now able to take – *Treasure Island* was short, *Dr Jekyll and Mr Hyde* a mere novella, and *Kidnapped* broken off very suddenly from a much larger project – he figured in the new order more by accident than design. By virtue of his career and romantic situation he was the biggest personality of them all. However, the sales he made and the fraternity which jealously guarded his reputation were different from the norms established by the commercial criteria of the new order.

We can, I think, claim too much for Stevenson as a popular author. Until after his death, his sales were sizeable but not start-ling. English editions of *Treasure Island* sold roughly 4,500 a year between 1883 and 1897, and the figures for *Catriona* and *The Master of Ballantrae* were similar. This was enough for a book to make a substantial impact on the book-buying public, but it was still well under the sort of market enjoyed by Dickens: *Bleak House* sold 35,000 in 1852–3. Even in the 1880s, with *Treasure Island, Dr Jekyll and Mr Hyde* and *Kidnapped* in print, Mrs Humphry Ward's worthy if scarcely thrilling celebration of the Oxford virtues of T. H. Green and Arnold Toynbee (thinly dis-guised), *Robert Elsmere*, could still sell 10,500 between 1888 and 1891.[2] So the notion of Stevenson's instant réclame with a whole generation of schoolboy readers will have to be revised though, be it noted, a book presumed to have had a similar effect on the young, Tom Hughes's *Tom Brown's Schooldays* (1857) had an annual sale which was roughly similar. At least during his lifetime, his appeal – both in Britain and America – was to the 'classes' rather than the 'masses' – a market which could latterly provide him with the reasonable income of £1,000 a year, on a relatively modest circula-tion.[3]

I think Stevensonianism must bear analysis, as well as Stevenson himself. I want to argue that, in part, his reputation grew because it accorded with developments within the literary society of his time: influential groups had motives of their own for patronising him, as well as appreciation of his distinctive qualities. And then, in a broader – and possibly more debateable – sense that the sombre subject-matter of the later novels was to some extent due to the interaction of Stevenson's own powerful personal preoccupations with those of a predominantly middle-class critical coterie and readership.

The 'Stevensonians' of the 1880s and 1890s can I think be divided into three, or possibly four groups. First, the academic *littérateurs*; secondly, the 'rolled up sleeves' school of 'masculine' journalism; thirdly, the Scots – with an internal division between the Conservatives and the Kailyarders. Each had different perceptions of the author, and each perception hinged on a somewhat different literary-political stance.

First, the 'high-minded' academics, Brahmins, or what have you: not hitherto a group much given to trifling with the sort of fare that Stevenson purveyed, yet providing in Sidney Colvin, Leslie Stephen, Edmund Gosse and Henry James some of his earliest and most resolute champions. Their attitudes were, I think, related to two main factors: the shift of academic interest away from the political arena in the 1870s and 1880s, and the attempt to make the academic study of literature respectable. Certain aspects of the academic style were immediately receptive to the Stevensonian ethos: academic liberals of the 1860s were 'masculine' and adventurous; in G. M. Young's words, 'men in tweeds who smoke in the street', given to mountain-climbing, long walks in remote areas, participation in – or at least observation of – foreign upheavals. Yet always, at their back, was that image of secure conviviality we get in Stevenson: good food and wine and the fellowship of their colleges.[4]

Yet the atmosphere that Stevenson's 'academic' advocates had been reared in was also a taxing and ultimately frustrating one: that of the strife-ridden 1860s, when most of them had been committed to the liberation of learning and research from clerical control. This was part of a greater political commitment to political democracy and economic individualism, and to a sociological understanding, albeit based on a fairly narrow rationalist base. Academically, this had issued in debate between the supporters of specialism and research, and those who believed in the efficacy of the essentially gymnastic training offered by the conventional courses at Oxford and Cambridge. One of the crucial issues in dispute was the teaching of modern literature as a major university subject. This split the liberals, and saw Benjamin Jowett, their Oxford leader, at his most authoritarian in his dismissal of the Shakespearian critic,

A. C. Bradley, in 1881. Thus, in the absence of formal training and research schools, the self-confidence of the liberal advocates of English as a literary discipline required reassurance.

It's evident that, by the 1870s, the enthusiasm of the more literary of the academic liberal group for politics was dwindling fast. Leslie Stephen – an early patron of Stevenson – is a case in point. In the 1860s he had been a militant academic reformer and democrat, a contributor to *Essays on Reform* in 1867, who came close to a parliamentary candidature. By the mid-1870s, as his regular dispatches to the New York *Nation* indicate, affairs of state were becoming, at best, a bore, and at worst a moral menace, 'Isn't politics always a rather mean pursuit?'[5] he observed to his more sanguine cousin, A. V. Dicey, who took over his column. By 1886 both men were, with varying degrees of enthusiasm, enrolled, along with Stevenson, Henley and Colvin in the ranks of the Unionists, and the same could be said of most of those who were their colleagues in the 1860s. The only prophylactic against such conservatism was direct involvement in the political process itself.

This disillusion with politics could manifest itself in conservatism or quietism, or in a growing professionalism. The last involved the development of the academic study of literature. Accompanying this went a stress on those aspects which marked literary skill off from the study of politics or history. As Walter Raleigh, author of one of the first studies of Stevenson (1895) and the younger brother of an Oxford liberal who subsequently became a prominent academic Unionist, put it to Edward Garnett in May 1889:

> I'm a good deal puzzled – and the question is now a very practical one for me – to get a comfortable or permanent niche in the order of things in general for literary criticism. If it is simply tracing literary cause and effect, as history is said to be the tracing of political cause and effect, I do not see why a lover of literature should go on to it any more than I see why a lover of painting should study chemistry.[6]

Raleigh, who had joined Bob Stevenson at Liverpool in 1890, was Merton Professor of English Literature at Oxford between 1905 and 1922; in 1912 Arthur Quiller-Couch ('Stevenson is dead: there is no one left to write for'), who completed *St Ives*, was appointed to the Cambridge chair in 1912, holding it until 1944. Both men, Unionists in 1886, later reverted to a high-minded Whiggish liberalism. 'Style', therefore, was not simply a literary affectation: it was a political declaration – not far from 'art for art's sake' – a move away

from a 'high seriousness' which found itself more and more per-
plexed by an intractable political situation.

If it was men from this background, notably Stephen and Sidney
Colvin, who first gave Stevenson his chance as a belle-lettrist, his
reputation was reinforced by a group on their fringes which publi-
cised him in a much more aggressive if haphazard way, the 'men of
letters'. This group was the result of expansion in the educational
system (the public rather than the elementary schools) as well as,
to a lesser extent, the growth of journalism. At one level, so
blurred were the frontiers, they were scarcely to be distinguished
from the academics (Churton Collins, the great proponent of the
academic study of literature, certainly had his own fierce criteria,
but academic society disowned him), at the other end they shaded
off into the penny-a-line miseries of Gissing's *New Grub Street*.
Gissing symbolised their feelings about R.L.S. by bursting out in
1888: 'A paper [by Henry James] on Stevenson I cannot read;
my prejudice against the man is insuperable, inexplicable, painful;
I hate to see his name, and certainly shall never bring myself to
read one of his books. Don't quite understand the source of this
feeling.'[7]

But this was not all; there was an enormous expansion in middle-
brow journalism as a whole: partly this was to do with a larger
literate public; partly to do with the lessening hold of religious
controversy. Boy's, women's and specialist magazines multiplied,
and literature itself began to cater for the 'fan' as well as the critical
market, one which was growing rapidly as the grip of the lending
libraries and the three-volume novel declined.[8] Partially this drew
on a recrudescent Bohemia (one suspects that the 1860s, the great
years of donnish journalism, were rather dull for the uninitiated
and apolitical) and also, in another direction, from the underem-
ployed ranks of the clergy, both established and nonconformist.
The clergy will come later, when we look at the Scottish contribution, but Stevenson as a cause could unite the would-be academics
like Edmund Gosse with the shirt-sleeved school, personified by
W. E. Henley. It wasn't a one way traffic, of course! Stevenson was
closer to Bohemia than he would ever be to academia (although he
got references for his Edinburgh chair bid in 1883 from various
respectable figures who should have known better). Mutual appreciation thrived on a diet of talk, burgundy and cigarettes. Yet there
was logic to Bohemia; given his perilous health and frequent
moves, Stevenson needed a literary agent, and was fortunate that
Bohemia served his purposes – at least until Fanny came along.

This was characteristic of the time; an earlier generation of authors were much more in the hands of their publishers; a later generation were similarly reliant on their agents. And Bohemia, as Stevenson found with Henley, could be embarrassingly disorganised. But on the whole it worked out to mutual advantage, and few who had linked their names with his would lack for future employment in one division or another of the Stevenson industry.

The men of letters shared with their eighteenth-century pre-cursors a common problem of living by the pen. This meant that they were sensitive to changes in the literary market and, although they might have strong political feelings, what mattered was cheques. The literary and political changes of the 1880s had affected this group most rapidly. Here, as in academic life, liberalism was beginning to be at a discount – possibly anticipated by W. H. Smith himself, who resigned the Liberal whip in 1865 and in 1868 beat John Stuart Mill at Westminster. Middle-class businessmen, sup-porters of the Liberal party as the upholder of 'sound finance' and minimal expenditure, were, as the behaviour of the City and sub-urbs showed, shifting to the Conservatives. For the commentator who followed his pocket, patronage was now coming from the right, and for the man of radical principle, there was so much unsatisfactory about the Liberal party that, all things being equal, he would rather work for a competent right-wing boss than an incompetent left-winger.

The men of letters were close enough to the political wind to be swayed by it, and Henley was a particularly – almost absurdly – fierce right-wing partisan. But in this he reflected a general shift to the right in the literary world in the 1880s. A Liberal propaganda book, *Why I am a Liberal*, published just before the General Election of 1885 claimed Leslie Stephen, Huxley, Tennyson, Browning and Matthew Arnold as Liberal supporters; a year later all of these had become Unionist over Gladstone's home rule policy. Meredith virtually alone of the big names, remained a Liberal. Stevenson, fundamentally always a Tory, did his bit for journalistic Unionism when in 1887 he dreamed up a crazy scheme of moving his whole family to Ireland to take the place of a boycot-ted Tipperary family and thus defy the Parnellites.[9] Remarkable copy for Henley's *Scots Observer*, but scarcely likely to enhance Stevenson's oddly apolitical reputation. I say oddly advisedly, be-cause of what I am going to argue in the final section of this paper, namely, that Stevenson is much more logically conservative than we generally credit him with being. And yet his reputation is on the whole a liberal one. I recollect a fulsome collection of essays prefaced by Isaac Foot, M.P., that pillar of West Country radicalism,[10] and I have just seen a film of a Communist May Day march in Glasgow in 1938 in which a huge banner of Stevenson shares pride of place with Burns and Wallace, Marx and Lenin. To understand this particular image, I believe we have to look at the third group of Stevenson partisans: the Scots. Even here I think we have to make a distinction: there was one group of Scots with whom Stevenson had distinct social affiliations, and another which used him, quite unscrupulously, to engineer its own legitimacy. The first was Edinburgh-based and Tory; the second London-based and Liberal.

Stevenson was, by birth, a Scottish Tory, and since the days of Scott the Scots Tories had claimed to represent an imaginative and literate – if not politically effective – response to the dull religious sectarianism of the Liberals. They could still pride themselves on a shadowy Jacobite prehistory; on being the party of Galt, Chalmers, Hogg, Aytoun and Lockhart, and the bibulous pundits of *Noctes Ambrosiana*; on a love of truth, wit and style, and a hatred of Pharasaism and humbug. Even Thomas Stevenson, with his eccentric religious opinions, comes closer to the personality of this tradition than to the Gradgrindery of, say, Lord Provost Duncan Maclaren, nineteenth-century Scotland's leading Liberal. By the 1880s something of this was visible in parliament in Arthur Balfour, Stevensonian in name and delicate figure, and in the tough and resilient politician thus concealed. John Connell, in his study of W. E. Henley, has described the cultivated society that Stevenson quitted for the South Seas:

> They were well-to-do. They lived spaciously in big town houses in Edinburgh; and they had shooting-lodges or deer forests in the Highlands . . . the rift which developed in the Eighties and the Nineties between the hearties and the aesthetes in England seemed then nonsensical; but they were also, apt to read and argue, at length, about French or German poetry; they were instructed about pictures and furniture and fine painting; in things of the mind they were eager and exploratory, and politically they were realistic and unequivocal. Staunchly Conservative and Unionist, they were animated by a sturdy, intelligent vigorous scepticism about the flabby theories in politics which were then becoming fashionable.[11]

The Edinburgh Tories – Henry Grey Graham, Sir Henry Craik, Charles Baxter, the backers of the *Scots Observer* – are a neglected group, although they were competent administrators, patrons and historians, and greatly responsible for reviving the study of the eighteenth-century enlightenment, providing an elite justification for the Union, now increasingly criticised from a home rule standpoint. Stevenson owed them more than they owed him.

It was quite other with the Kailyarders, whose rise was, in the 1880s, even more spectacular. Robertson Nicoll and his followers, mainly Free Church clergymen, milked Stevenson for all he was worth. There are several gluey anthologies along 'what R.L.S. meant to me' lines, culled from the pages of the *British Weekly* or *The Bookman*. Privately, Nicoll, although he used a Stevenson article to open an early number of the *British Weekly*, did not care for Stevenson in the least. As he wrote to Marcus Dods in May 1887:

> I am glad you liked R.L.Stevenson, but these articles make little difference to the sale. It is personal matter that people like. Don't you think there is something sickly about R.L.S. – perfume at best, opium at worst? He is not *fresh* in the right way, is he? I think Mark Rutherford a much greater master of English style.[12]

Yet Stevenson was a valuable property, and at one level the influence of this clique probably helped turn his mind more and more from the South Seas to Scotland and 'the book that is in him' – in Barrie's words. We know that from his heartfelt poem 'To S.R. Crockett' (1894). Whatever else it did, the Kailyarders' portrayal of Scotland had certainly made the country marketable, after a lapse of some fifty years since the death of Scott. The image they had refurbished of the country, moreover, was essentially the child-centred one of the exile: the Scotland of school, kirk and small community, a 'Gemeinschaft' in which the growing polarities of politics and society could be resolved, albeit in an age when experience of the quiet places of the exiles' Scotland was outweighed, for the mass of the population, by the slums of Kilmarnock or Dundee.

The Kailyarders were political Liberals, and many of them were quite subtle and sophisticated Liberals, disciples of T.H.Green, sponsors of a new social politics in Church and State. To them Stevenson's revolt against the old rigidities of mid-nineteenth-century religious politics, his sympathy for children, his championing of effective values in education, reinforced their own aims. As late as 1945 Jimmie Maxton, an archetypal Kailyard radical, was arguing in the House of Commons that Stevenson's essays contained the essential programme of child-centred education in Scotland. The Kailyarders wanted moderate reform to be achieved out of good feeling, floated in on a tide of nostalgia and sentiment, and a selective reading and repetition of Stevenson, whom they knew had much more class than they could ever manage, served their cause well.

Moving from coterie to writer, there was at least a radical aspect, or rather phase, to Stevenson. In the early 1870s – his Edinburgh pub-crawling phase – he advertised himself as a socialist and republican, probably under the influence of the Paris commune as well as the religious feud with his father. It is difficult to provide an intellectual pedigree beyond the rather contradictory figures of Walt Whitman and Herbert Spencer. There was certainly a lot of quasi-Swinburnian excess around at that time. Edward Carpenter, another Whitmanite, remembered a Cambridge contemporary writing a piece of atheistic doggerel which began

Oh Father, Son and Holy Ghost,
We wonder which we hate the most . . .[13]

It didn't last. It had probably evaporated, even before his reconciliation with his parents in the late 1870s took him back to the family Toryism. Two things remained: his religious unbelief, and an imaginative sympathy – not so much with the poor *per se*, as with their attitude to the rich. Witness this passage in *The Amateur Emigrant*:

Through this merry and good-hearted scene there come three cabin passengers, a gentleman and two young ladies, picking their way with little gracious titters of indulgence, and a Lady Bountiful air about nothing, which galled me to the quick. I have little of the radical in social questions, and have always nourished an idea that one person was as good as another. But I began to be troubled by this episode. It was astonishing what insults these people managed to convey by their presence.[14]

For the rest, he became a solidly anti-Gladstonian Tory whose hostility to Liberalism, while less rancid than, say, Rudyard Kipling's, far pre-dated the split of 1886.

Stevenson, I've suggested, was remote from the gravitas of 'the great tradition', yet in 1873, during this radical phase, he met and was deeply influenced by one writer who was much more political than many within the tradition. Doris Lessing has remarked on the absence of the 'metropolitan' novel in nineteenth-century Britain: Hardy and George Eliot were self-consciously provincial, Dickens's London was an idiosyncratic creation; British novelists were, as a whole, innocent of any great interest in European affairs. The exception to this is George Meredith, and this may account for

the continuing interest he provokes among academics, in the absence of any widespread popularity.[15] Meredith was radical, cosmo-
politan, and deeply conscious of a duty to interpret the sweep of
social change. G. M. Trevelyan wrote of his study of the 1848 revo-
lutions in Italy, *Vittoria* (1867): 'It is not only a great prose poem
on an epic moment in human affairs, but a detailed and accurate
analysis of a people and of a period.'[16] It was under Meredith's
influence that Stevenson expended great pains, between 1880 and
1886, on his one serious novel about contemporary politics, *Prince
Otto*.

Prince Otto (1885) is generally treated as an 'out-of-character'
mistake, like its contemporary, James's *The Princess Casamassima*
(1886). Yet both books were written when their authors were
discussing the theory of the novel and its relation to reality, and
although both men moved into fields equally remote from the
'political novel', these two works define in a sense their reasons for
distancing themselves from contemporary politics at a crucial 'Zeit-
bruch': that period, during the mid-1880s, when the overthrow of
middle-class society, and the imposition of a socialist order,
seemed for the first time to become a possibility.

The political crisis sorted itself out. The forces of the left were
given a sharp setback by the events of 1886 – the collapse of Irish
home rule – and the subsequent twenty-year Conservative hegemony: the fear (expressed in some of Stevenson's unpublished
political writings) that the drift was inescapably to socialism and
violence, was allayed.[17] But it seemed a close-run thing, achieved
by luck as well as the acumen of the political establishment, and
both the framework of the adventure-novel, in Stevenson, and the
aristocratic/plutocratic human comedy of James are set in relief by
realising that they had glanced from the stage into the nearby, very
deep, pit. James summed up the problem, at the end of *The Princess Casamassima*, when his hero Hyacinth turns from the revolution to suicide, in terms which describe the politics of the adven-
ture-story, as well as those of the society James was henceforth to
revolve in:

> In these hours the poverty and ignorance of the multitude
> seemed so vast and preponderant, and so much the law of life,
> that those who had managed to escape from the black gulf were
> the happy few, people of resource as well as children of luck:
> they inspired in some degree the interest and sympathy that
> one should feel for survivors and victors, those who have come
> safely out of a shipwreck or a battle.[18]

So *Prince Otto*, which can claim some descent from Meredith's *Harry Richmond* (1871), has claims to contemporary political understanding. The year of the action, like that of *Vittoria*, is 1848. Sir John Crabtree, the cold, growling English Benthamite, who provides a documentary basis for Grunewald, is typical enough of itinerant Liberal commentators of the time. The Grunewald revolution goes the way of the Frankfurt parliament, and Gondremark ends in exile in Naples. Stevenson could have culled further from subsequent German history: the dotty aesthetic patronage and reckless behaviour of Ludwig II of Bavaria (1846–85), the role at his court in the 1860s of Richard Wagner, the North German protestant magus, ultimately forced from Bavaria in 1870. Yet the central figures exhibit an ambiguity which gives parallels with Jekyll and Hyde. Gondremark, the leader of the radicals and socialists, is also an authoritarian Caesarist, inveigling his supporters into wars of conquest in the interests of what looks like a sort of Napoleonic military despotism. Yet he is still a sympathetic creature, and it's quite understandable that his mistress drops Prince Otto like a hot brick when news comes of Gondremark's wounding at the hands of the princess. It is then time for these two other scattered personalities, the prince and princess, to achieve a unity of personality (albeit not of any great personality) and sexual fulfilment at the end of the novel. And there's a sense of personal identification in the modest farewell: 'Here, at least, we may take leave of Otto and Seraphina – what do I say? of Frédéric and Amélie – ageing together peaceably at the court of the wife's father, jingling French rhymes and correcting joint proofs.'[19]

If we compare *Prince Otto* with another romance of a small German state, Thomas Mann's *Royal Highness* (1912) I think we find the first more realistic. Both are elegies for the old Germany of woods and inns and slow good feeling, and something of the brutality of the Bismarckian Reich is visible in *Prince Otto*, for example, in Crabtree's description of Gondremark: 'He has called out the whole capable male population of the state to military service; he has cannons; he has tempted away promising officers from foreign armies; and he now begins in his international relations, to assume the swaggering part and the vague threatful language of the bully.'[20] Towards the end of his life Stevenson was to have to cope with this German *realpolitik* in Samoa. Mann's happy solution for royal Germany – meaningless constitutional monarchy given life and sympathy by marriage with American money – was a luxury Stevenson didn't allow himself, and Mann himself would

ultimately come to regret. The move within *Prince Otto* is a move
away from politics towards personal authenticity. Further, politics
are increasingly seen as distorting, untrue and dangerous. Yet
Stevenson's own development was not, I think, towards indivi-
dualist escapism, jingling French rhymes, but via the adventure
story, to something much tougher. Something much tougher: but
not the analysis of the fissured society of his native land which, in
the age of Zola and Ibsen, we might expect. Like his academic
patrons Stevenson was repelled by the realist novel. Not so much,
one suspects, because of the crudity of the subject-matter (at the
end of his life he regretted his failure as a writer to come to terms
with sex) but because the only possible resolution of the social
problems disclosed in the realistic novel seemed to imply some
appalling social upheaval. Yet, if we see in *Dr Jekyll and Mr Hyde* a
subsconscious metaphor for Stevenson's Scotland – its religiose
bourgeoisie and teeming slums – can a parallel theme not be
detected in his later fiction?

Stevenson's debate with James led an earlier generation of critics to
stress the polarities of 'romance' and 'realism'. Even today his
definition of the novel as 'neat, finite, self-contained, rational,
flowing and emasculate' has plainly attractions for modern struc-
turalists. But how pre-meditated were these values? How much did
Stevenson actually adhere to them? Or how much did the 'brute
energy, the inarticulate thunder' of real life, real politics, break
in?[21] Certainly in Stevenson's later novels there is a tension,
rarely satisfactorily resolved, between romantic pattern and, if not
reality, then some powerful projection of human nature, usually
repressed. And I would argue that both elements – of 'adventure',
and human nature – are used by Stevenson to sanction an overall
vision of society, which is firmly held, if never actually made
explicit.

The nineteenth-century boys' adventure story had a didactic,
conservative impulse analogous to that sympathy for the 'happy
few' evidenced by James. Its rewards were those offered by a stable
society: financial security, if the hero survived, the conferment of
moral worth, if he died bravely. The 'adventurer' and the romantic
criminal – the highwayman, for example – with their satisfactions
of momentary affluence or sex, were dislodged from a position they
had earlier held in polite literature. There is not much room in the
late nineteenth century for someone as amiably amoral as Barry
Lyndon, although cruder versions of him still survived in the

undergrowth of the 'penny dreadfuls'. Stevenson's criminals are not at all romantic – the pirates in *Treasure Island* and *The Master of Ballantrae*, the Irish terrorists in *The Dynamiter*, are realistically drunken and repellent, although the ostensible heroes are worthy and resourceful in the manner of Marryat, Ballantyne and Henty. In this sense the stories of Jim Hawkins or David Balfour were appropriate pabulum for the middle-class child whom the educational system enjoined to be manly and plucky (frequently with practical ends in view), and even the appearance alongside them of more ambiguous adult figures – the attractive rogue (Silver) and the gallant with weaknesses (Alan Breck) were useful means of throwing the youth's necessary transition to 'independence' into relief. What, however, constitutes Stevenson's fascination is the welling-up of powerful figures from the subconscious which distort this simple didacticism, in much the same way that Jekyll's attempt to eliminate his animal impulses produced Hyde. This dark side to Stevenson, which surely climaxed in *The Master of Ballantrae*, in which the central figure is neither hero nor rogue, but a figure both attractive and terrifyingly evil, has usually been seen as the function of his own history and personality. I don't want to detract from this but to suggest that it gains force when seen in terms of a social reality, which cut across and ultimately replaced the structure of the 'romance'.

Sir James Fitzjames Stephen, Leslie's lawyer brother, had a story about shipwrecked seamen drifting in an open boat through a remote archipelago. They were fearful of being murdered if they made a landfall, but then were given confidence by a familiar object on a headland – a gallows: evidence of the rule of law. Professor John Roach has argued that this tough-minded 'old Liberalism' was in the early 1880s gathering its strength for a last defence of its position, which the Liberal split of 1886 ultimately enabled.[22] Indeed the subsequent Unionist hegemony led directly to, in Lord Salisbury's words, 'the awakening of the slumbering genius of Imperialism', and to the authoritarianism imaginatively projected by Rudyard Kipling.

Now, I think that there is a parallel in Stevenson to this: from *Treasure Island* on, there is a mounting preoccupation with punishment and physical death, which goes beyond Stevenson's Fat Boy-like fascination with 'making your flesh creep'. As various commentators have remarked, his handling of the supernatural is a conjuring trick: there is no sense that rational causality could actually be overthrown in the real world. He seems, unlike various

of his contemporaries – such as Arthur Balfour and Henry Sidgwick
– to have been relatively uninterested in psychical research as a
basis for serious philosophical and psychological investigation.

In *Prince Otto,* which is after all about a revolution, violence
scarcely raises its head. The toughest character in the book, Major
Gordon, is a refined Scots literary gent. Hardly a thimbleful of
blood is spilt. Yet even in an entertainment like *Treasure Island*
there is death, and realistic death, aplenty : Bill Bones toppled by a
stroke, Pew crushed underfoot, Silver's brutal dispatch of the loyal
sailor, the bodies of Israel Hands and his victim, clearly visible on
the bed of the lagoon. Each death has its own character, yet each is
also seen against the two polarities of Long John Silver's own
relationship with death. As Jim Hawkins overhears in the apple-
barrel, the elimination of the Squire and his party is necessary to
make Silver not simply rich, but an M.P., a member of the British
establishment :

> 'If I had my way, I'd have Cap'n Smollet work us back into the
> trades at least ; then we'd have no blessed miscalculations and a
> spoonful of water a day. But I know the sort you are. I'll finish
> with 'em at the island, as soon as the blunt's on board, and a
> pity it is. But you're never happy until you're drunk. Split my
> sides, I've sick heart to sail with the likes of you !' . . .
> . . . 'Well, what would you think? Put 'em ashore like
> maroons? What would you think? That would have been Eng-
> land's way. Or cut 'em down like that much pork? That would
> have been Flint's or Billy Bones's. . . . But mark you here : I'm
> an easy man – I'm quite the gentleman, says you ; but this time
> it's serious. Dooty is dooty, mates. I give my vote – death.
> When I'm in Parlyment, and riding in my coach, I don't want
> none of these sea-lawyers in the cabin a 'coming home, un-
> looked-for, like the devil at prayers. Wait is what I say, but
> when the time comes, why, let her rip !'[23]

At the other polarity is society's defence from the likes of Silver,
deterrence by social vengeance : the corpses rotting in chains at
Execution Dock. There is a sense in which *Treasure Island* could
be seen as a sort of social parable : an embattled microcosm of civil
society – squire, doctor, captain and retainers – being menaced by
the lower orders under brutal and materialistic leadership. That the
establishment is saved by chance and Jim Hawkins shows the close
margin, although the propensity of the pirates (like the Edinburgh
working class Stevenson knew) to get smashed out of their minds
obviously helped. Silver ends up in the position of some teetotal

Jacobin, trying (unsuccessfully) to get his mob out of the pubs and on to the streets, and like all unsuccessful Jacobins in Britain – Ernest Jones, James Maxton, Willie Gallagher – gets spared and becomes a 'character'. It may be flippant, but the fact that *Treasure Island* appealed to adults as well as children suggests a certain affinity with the squire's embattled party among those groups who were on 8 February 1886 to have their club windows smashed by mobs rioting in the West End, or feared for their Irish properties as cattle-maiming and 'moonlighting' increased. With, added to this, the feeling that one or two Silvers had already made it to the House of Commons?

This brings us to *Dr Jekyll and Mr Hyde*: by far the most influential of Stevenson's 'psychological' fiction – on, for instance, Gide and Mann. The story came to Stevenson partly in a dream, partly through conscious developments of themes raised by earlier Scots authors such as Lockhart in *Adam Blair* and Hogg in *The Confessions of a Justified Sinner*. Yet is there not also an input from contemporary history? Gladstone, whom Stevenson loathed, had a nocturnal existence as the 'rescuer' of London prostitutes. These bedraggled sparrows were taken back and fed on cocoa and tracts by Mrs Gladstone, although Tory gossip supposed otherwise. (Indeed Gladstone's motivation was ambiguous and, as the recent publication of his diaries has shown, mixed up with his problem of equating his religious fervour with his powerful sexual drive, which earlier had led him to self-flagellation.)[24] Stevenson, given his London journalistic contacts, probably knew about this, but more important was the political aspect. Gladstone, the public exemplification of Christian high-minded politics, had in Stevenson's eyes, allowed the murder at Khartoum of General Gordon, in 1885. He had also become, in 1885, the ally of the Irish political party, through his adoption of home rule. By this step, in Tory eyes, he was condoning the campaign of agrarian violence launched by adherents of the Land League and sanctioned by the Irish M.P.s at Westminster. More crucially – again this was a theme in Tory gossip which was to surface in *The Times'* notorious series 'Parnellism and Crime' in April 1887 – his new Irish ally had been privy to the terroristic campaigns of the early 1880s, which Stevenson himself implies in his preface to *The Dynamiter*.[25] And the horrifying climax of this terrorism had been the murder of the Irish Chief Secretary, Lord Frederick Cavendish, and his senior administrator, Thomas Burke, in Phoenix Park, Dublin, on 6 May 1882, an event which, as James Bryce recollected, sent a horror through

English political society which was not to be equalled until August 1914. Hence the human dualism of *Dr Jekyll and Mr Hyde* is not, I suspect, simply of psychological interest; it appealed to the book-reading public because it provided a parable as well as a convenient metaphor for the politics of their time.

The theme of primitive evil is also an important one in con-servative thought in the 1880s. Liberals had assumed that human character was a given quality, to be moulded by environment and education. It was in the 1880s that they began to realise the magni-tude of the task thus posed. Commenting on three conservative novels of 1886 – Mallock's *The Old Order Changes,* Gissing's *Demos* and James's *The Princess Casamassima* – John Lucas has noted how the fear inspired by the growth of a socialist movement was mingled with a realisation that artistic and literary culture had always been the province of a minority, and would inevitably be a casualty. Moreover, underlying this, there was a horrifying void of information about what the working class was actually like.[26] In this context, the rioting which broke out after a demonstration on unemployment in February 1886, the stoning and looting of West End clubs, seemed a terrifying glimpse, not of a socialist revolu-tion, but of mindless and destructive atavism. As Gareth Stedman Jones has shown in *Outcast London,* the educated classes sub-sequently came to think that any form of working-class organisa-tion, even socialism, was preferable to this Jacquerie. Hence Toyn-bee Hall.[27] More robust spirits on the right reached for law and the rope. It was against this dehumanisation and frightening polarisa-tion that the mild reformists of the Kailyard took refuge in their provincial security 'where a'body knew a'body'.

Thus there are in the later Stevenson two themes which he finds increasingly difficult to relate to the patterns of romance: the theme of justice and punishment, and the theme of human evil. *Kid-napped/Catriona* hinges on the Appin murder and its consequen-ces; *The Master of Ballantrae* on the capacity of evil to triumph over good, and *Weir of Hermiston* on the clash of judicial integrity with personal feelings. In the case of all three the weight of this moral issue, and Stevenson's very skill in presenting it, distorts the 'romantic' pattern of the novel.

I believe that we must see *Weir of Hermiston,* which has been claimed as Stevenson's masterpiece, in this context: as a conserva-tive parable of law and duty, as well as a conscious shift into that historically dominated environment redolent of Scott. Curiously, and in a sort of half-tribute to the Kailyard, as well as to Scott, the

theme of evil is exorcised – even Frank Innes would be no match
for the Master – to be replaced by recognisable human attributes:
the straightforward sexuality of the younger Kirstie, and the more
ambivalent feelings of the older, the chorus of contemporary Scotland set up by the 'Four Black Brothers' – radical visionary weaver,
'improving' farmer, businessman and poet – and above all the
embodiment of the old Scotland in Hermiston himself. Braxfield
had attracted Stevenson as early as the mid-1870s, and his first
encounter is well told in 'Some Portraits by Raeburn'. From this,
Stevenson's mind proceeded on 'romantic plotting' lines, much as
it had done with *The Master of Ballantrae*, leaving us of course
with the problem – would Stevenson have a romantic ending for the
Saturnian tragedy for which his characterisation of the judge prepares us? And yet, even if Archie and Kirstie escaped, would the
death of Hermiston not be tragedy enough?

The charge that can be made against Stevenson is the one that
Georg Lukacs levelled against the Thomas Mann of *Buddenbrooks*
and *Royal Highness*: through sympathetic literary presentation
giving 'composure' to an otherwise unacceptable political order.[28]
Braxfield – accepted as the greatest feudal lawyer of his day – was by
any standards a partisan judge. 'Certainly, I am afraid he was inhumane' writes Stevenson in 1876 – 'a living embodiment of the
counter-revolution'. Yet, unquestionably, Weir towers over every
other character in the book: morally as well as in terms of personality. He crushes Jopp as if he were a beetle, but Stevenson
doesn't imply the least miscarriage of justice – or anything remotely
un-beetle like about Jopp. As for Archie's revulsion against capital
punishment, we don't get a syllable of argument in its favour at the
Speculative Society, and then he breaks down and blubs in front of
his father. As a figure of autochthonous charismatic power, Weir
invites comparison with Henchard in *The Mayor of Casterbridge*,
but the flaw which will produce personal collapse isn't there.
Nothing in Weir's character suggests that he will ever betray his
concept of justice even if the cost is his son's life and his own.
Climbing 'the great staircase of his duty' he, in a social context, is a
figure as powerfully and sympathetically symbolic as that other
Scot, the dour, boring Macwhirr on the bridge of the *Nan-Shan* in
Conrad's *Typhoon* (1903).

In the context of the moral landscape of Stevenson's last works
the emergence of several such figures is significant. One could call
them 'superior mercenaries', willing, without much enthusiasm,
to 'save the sum of things for pay'. For, just as in stories like *The*

Ebb Tide and *The Wrecker* Stevenson showed the destructive potential of fairly ordinary, un-demonic humanity (and surely he never wrote anything more horrible than the slaughter of the crew of the *Flying Scud*) he enhances the status of the capable, mercenary lawman, the essential policeman of Herbert Spencer's minimal state. Captain Nares, in *The Wrecker,* is of this type, and there is something of Weir in the documentary sketch in the same book of William Tell Coleman, who had led the San Francisco Vigilantes in the 1850s, and whose reputation was sufficient to quell the potential outbreak of proletarian violence of the Kearneyites in the same city in the 1870s:

> That lion of the Vigilantes had but to rouse himself and shake his ears, and the whole brawling mob was silenced. . . . In a thousand towns and different epochs I might have had occasion to behold the cowardice and carnage of street fighting; where else, but only there and then, could I have enjoyed a view of Coleman (the intermittent despot) walking meditatively up hill in a quiet part of town, with a very rolling gait, and slapping gently his great thigh?[29]

So that ultimately Stevenson's political creed is authoritarian but – unlike Kipling – feudal and familial rather than technocratic. Weir was an image of the power of that legal system which underlay the Scots enlightenment, yet which was drawn from a pre-existent social state not unlike that which Stevenson himself tried to recreate in Samoa: a charismatic authority now being sapped by imperialist bureaucrats as much as by socialistic bureaucrats at home. Which may, in a sense, provide an answer to the question: why didn't Stevenson tackle the social realities of Scotland of his own day? He knew enough about the low life of the place. He knew how distorted the Kailyard view of it was. But, as a conservative, admittedly of a fairly visceral sort, he also knew the potential for chaos that boiled below the surface. *Weir of Hermiston* is an attempt to face up to the problems that realism exposed by 'composing' the ability of law to control them and, if need be, suppress them.

References

1   See Adrian Poole, *Gissing in Context* (Macmillan 1975) 119; John Gross, *The Rise and Fall of the Man of Letters* (1969, Penguin 1973) 222-3.
2   Details of Stevenson's works from *British Museum Catalogue*; of other best-sellers from R. D. Altick, *The English Common Reader* (University of Chicago Press 1957) 383-6.
3   Stevenson's income according to J. C. Furnas in

Voyage to Windward (Faber 1952) 368.

4   For the academic liberals see the present writer's
    The Lights of Liberalism (Allen Lane 1976) 211-12.

5   Henry Jackson MS., Trinity College Cambridge,
    A. V. Dicey-Jackson, 21 February 1917; see also
    N. G. Annan, *Leslie Stephen* (MacGibbon and Kee
    1951) 60, and Harvie, op. cit., 225.

6   Quoted in D. J. Palmer, *The Rise of English Studies*
    (Oxford 1965) 121; and see Gross, op. cit., 198-209.

7   George Gissing, *Diary*, ed. F. C. Coustillas (Harvester
    Press 1978) 33 (entry for June, 1888). He got round to
    reading Stevenson in the nineties and commented in
    1902 : 'Was this mere jealousy? Of course I have long
    since ceased to be capable of such feeling.'

8   Altick, op. cit., 362-3.

9   Furnas, op. cit., 229-30.

10 Isaac Foot in *Robert Louis Stevenson: His Work and
    Personality* (Hodder and Stoughton 1924).

11 John Connell, *W. E. Henley* (Constable 1949) 136.

12 T. H. Darlow, *William Robertson Nicoll, his Life and
    Letters* (Hodder and Stoughton 1925) 76.

13 Edward Carpenter, *My Days and Dreams* (Allen &
    Unwin 1916) 60.

14 *The Amateur Emigrant* (1895) Pentland edition (1907)
    vol. II, 35. (All subsequent references to Stevenson's
    works are to this edition.)

15 Doris Lessing, 'Introduction' to *The Golden Notebook*
    (Panther edition 1965) 11.

16 G. M. Trevelyan, *England and Italy*, Proceedings of
    the British Academy (1919-20) 100-1.

17 See 'The Day after Tomorrow' in vol. 15, 310-21.

18 Henry James, *The Princess Casamassima* (Macmillan
    1948) vol. II, 235.

19 *Prince Otto*, vol. VII, 221.

20 ibid., 66-7.

21 See 'A Humble Remonstrance' (1884) in *Henry James
    and Robert Louis Stevenson*, ed. Janet Adam Smith
    (Hart-Davis 1948) 92.

22 John Roach, 'Liberalism and the Victorian Intelligent-
    sia', in *Cambridge Historical Journal* 13, 1957.

23 *Treasure Island*, vol. V, 87-8.

24 *The Gladstone Diaries*, ed. H. G. C. Matthew, vol. 3
    (Oxford University Press 1978).

25 Preface to *The Dynamiter*, vol. VI, 181-2.

26 John Lucas, 'Conservatism and Revolution in the
    1880s' in *Literature and Politics in the Nineteenth
    Century*, ed. J. Lucas (Methuen 1971) 173-220.

27 Stedman Jones, op. cit. (Macmillan 1975) 337-49.

28 G. Lukacs, 'In Search of Bourgeois Man' in *Essays on
    Thomas Mann* (Grosset and Dunlap 1965) 24-5.

29 *The Wrecker* (1892) vol. XII, 141.

J. C. FURNAS

Stevenson and Exile

I am asked to discuss 'Stevenson and Exile'. The Oxford English
Dictionary says that in the original, narrow sense exile means
something formally punitive: 'enforced removal from one's native
land according to an edict or sentence'. That fits the cases of several
literary figures I can think of, beginning with Ovid in classical
times, continuing with Villon in the Middle Ages; but not that of
Robert Louis Stevenson. At one point in his South Seas phase his
involvement in Samoan politics made it conceivable that the High
Commissioner of the Western Pacific, Sir John Thurston, might
order him deported as a meddlesome and seditious nuisance. It
deprived biographers of several dramatic pages when that severity
did not come to pass. Yet even had Sir John been so ill advised,
enforced removal of this irksome literary man would not have
amounted to exile within the meaning of the statute. Samoa was
not Louis Stevenson's native land. He was buried there. He was not
born there, and throughout his forty-four years the mark of Edinburgh particularly and of Scotland generally was strong on him – as
much more so when in exile as when his foot was on his native
heath – as several of my colleagues in this volume have already well
established.

The Oxford English Dictionary's second definition makes exile
'expatriation, prolonged absence from one's native land, endured
by compulsion of circumstances or voluntarily undergone for any
purpose'. That is more like it. Once Louis Stevenson attained his
majority, his absences from his native land account for roughly
four-fifths of the rest of his lamentably short life. Much France, a
little Germany, a little Switzerland, a certain amount of England,
two experiments with America, five years in the South Seas. . . . But
the dictionary is hardly needed. Toward the end of his life Louis
himself, a man careful of exact meanings, called his personal

situation *exile*. It is worth while, however, to explore to what extent 'compulsion of circumstances' entered into this matter. Its fruits were enjoyable for readers and those who relish contact with persons, dead or alive, who possess style and savor.

These are not simple issues, of course. Louis Stevenson was not a simple person. They lead into considerations carrying the stamp of his time and are closely related to trends in his life and work often regarded, sometimes justly, as romantic.

One guiding strand begins where he began—in Scotland, specifically with the Scottish climate. An American must tread warily here. His native environment—whether California or Minnesota or Virginia — is poor preparation for understanding the relations between Scots and their weather. I mention this the more reluctantly because during my several visits to Edinburgh over the last thirty years, the climate has usually treated me almost as well as its cordial people. Others at other times, however, including many Scots, have not been so fortunate. But none have outdone Louis in denunciations of Scotland's cutting winds and lashing rains and overcast skies. As a young health-seeker in the south of France Louis wrote shudderingly of 'the grim wintry streets at home. The hopeless, huddled attitudes of tramps in doorways; the flinching gait of barefoot children on the icy pavement; the sheen of the rainy streets toward afternoon; the meagre anatomy of the poor defined by the clinging of wet garments; the high canorous note of the Northeaster on days when the very houses seem to stiffen with cold.'[1]

He had particular cause to deplore all that because, whereas certain physical temperaments among Scots as elsewhere thrive in such environments, he had a significant family history of trouble in the upper respiratory tract. On his father's side the Stevenson dynasty of civil engineers who spent so much of their lives building lighthouses and harbor works in some of Scotland's bleakest and most blustery situations seems to have taken little harm. But Louis's maternal grandfather Balfour and his youngest daughter, Louis's mother, were both occasionally sent to winter in the Mediterranean climate because of over-susceptibility to chest ailments. The connection between climate and that ill understood group of diseases to which the human breathing apparatus is subject is not yet well established. But once matters grow chronic in the sinuses or the bronchi or the lung tissues, damp, windy, chilly conditions are traditionally – and probably soundly – assumed to be unfavorable. We have no reliable way to discover what turned Mrs Thomas

Stevenson's plump baby into a bony little half-invalid and then into
an illness-harried exile hoping for reasonable health – somewhere.
But his troubles usually centered on 'the bellows', that much is
clear. And other things being equal, Scotland is a poor place for
such.

Accordingly the child's first absences from Scotland, his proto-
exiles, so to speak, were health-seeking stays in Italy and on the
Riviera. At that time conscientious physicians had few reliable
means for either diagnosing or treating most diseases. 'Change of
air' was prescribed almost as freely as aspirin is now; that is, often
for lack of anything more promising to suggest. Climate was
specially relied on for 'delicate health', 'weak chest' – when using
those phrases our forebears had what they called 'consumption'
(pulmonary tuberculosis) in mind. Medicine now uses specific
drugs to control and often arrest it. But in the mid-1800s nobody
had even dreamed of isoniazid, and the search for effective treatment had led to a curious variety of trial and error measures. For a
while they recommended the vicinity of horses; the patient was
told to live over a stable and ride a great deal. Then it was sea
voyages. Then mild climates as aforesaid. Then high, dry mountain
air. Then the vicinity of pine woods, the scent of which was
thought to strengthen lung tissues. Note that in such contexts
affluence was implicit. Only the relatively well to do could afford to
leave home for winters in Italy or Provence or Switzerland. The
invalid's healthy spouse or parents or offspring who went along to
look after him often found it was much more pleasant there in
January than back home in Copenhagen or St Petersburg. Thus it
came about that this tradition of therapeutic exile for not only Scots
and English but also Germans, Scandinavians, Slavs, was the basis
on which the Riviera, Madeira and Switzerland-in-winter became
fashionable resorts for the healthy as well.

As treatment thus exiling the phthisical was not altogether non-
sense. The fewer winter colds such a case contracts, the better; and
Stevenson's devoted wife was well justified when insisting, in
advance of scientific knowledge, that nobody who could not show a
clean handkerchief should come near him. Further, pulmonary
tuberculosis, like many other complaints, seems to have a psycho-
logical-emotional element. It may be related to what doctors call
the 'placebo-effect'. They have only recently begun to understand
the biochemistry behind it. To give a chronic invalid plain sugar
pills or injections of distilled water and tell him impressively that
this is a new, probably sure-fire cure for what ails him often effects

striking improvement, for a while at least. In Louis Stevenson's time to ship a patient with 'weak lungs' to enjoy sunshine all winter at Nice with the assurance that it was the best possible measure sometimes effected an arrest. And that, of course, encouraged his doctor to send other such cases to the same place, and prepared potential patients to accept sentence of exile as the proper treatment.

Now translate the foregoing series of ill-founded but well-meant therapies into the relevant place names. Mild winter climate meant Menton and Hyères. High, dry mountain air meant Davos in Europe and the Adirondack Mountains in America. Pine woods meant Bournemouth. Sea-voyage meant the South Seas, first in a yacht and then in trading vessels. It is an epitome of much of Louis's adult life. Obviously the geographical-meteorological school of tuberculosis therapy exiled him from that native heath almost as drastically as if an early nineteenth-century judge, Lord Braxfield, say, had condemned him to transportation overseas for life. Even when, in his third decade, Louis tried summering in the Scottish Highlands, his frail bellows failed him. Bournemouth forced him into a virtual house-arrest. After that 3,000 miles for another trial of the mountain-air formula in the Adirondacks; and still another 3,000 to San Francisco and the chartered yacht and the South Seas where he found relative health – and died.

The sea-voyage method was assuredly best for this patient. He said he was never well except when at séa. He seems to have been immune to sea-sickness; whereas his indomitable wife was no great sailor. The Flying Dutchman was doomed to keep the high seas forever as punishment for blasphemously defying Providence. Edward Everett Hale's Man Without a Country was punished for abetting treason by lifelong transfer from one U.S. Navy vessel to another, never again setting foot on the land he had tried to betray. Those sentences to exile-at-sea were indeed severe but it may be doubted whether Stevenson would have found them purely intolerable. If exile it had to be, that was the kind he would probably have preferred, rather as Br'er Rabbit felt when he beguiled Br'er Fox into throwing him into the hospitable brier patch. Maybe physiologically as well as psychologically – if the two can be separated – his optimum destiny would have been that of a Flying Scot – not the famous train but a human organism self-committed to a buoyant life on saltwater, making port only for mail and supplies, including plenty of red wine and cigarette tobacco. For he was a chain-smoker and doctors did not yet appreciate how much that habit probably exacerbated his recurrent ailments.

Particularly in the Pacific, running down the northeast trade-winds, he was 'aware of a spiritual change or perhaps, rather, a molecular reconstruction. My bones were sweeter to me. I had come to my own climate, and looked back with pity on those damp and wintry zones miscalled the temperate. . . . The blank sea itself grew desirable . . . wherever the trade-wind blows, I know no better country than a schooner's deck.'[2] The vocabulary is almost clinical. The veteran invalid exults in finding, after so much waste motion, the right prescription. This experience at sea in the yacht set him more than half-seriously planning to buy a South Seas trading schooner to earn her own way and serve him as floating headquarters with occasional calls at commercial centers for restocking. The vessel was never bought. But the headquarters he did acquire, the inchoate plantation in Samoa that he named Vailima, lay high above the beach with the trade-wind whispering and filtering through the house and a vast view of the distant Pacific.

Now how voluntary can this fortunate exile be considered? There certainly was an element of compulsion by threat. In Samoa Louis spoke off and on of a trip home for at least temporary reunion with friends; or of arranging to meet some of them halfway in Madeira; even of trying a lecture-tour in the States. But each time he quitted Samoa, once for Hawaii, twice for Australia, old familiar ailments assailed him in even those mildish climates; whereas in Samoa he usually had what was for him almost good health. He worked outdoors, rode a good deal, actively partook in political and social affairs, wrote much and very well. Those insubstantial barriers, the Tropics of Capricorn and Cancer, menacingly marked the limits of his banishment as though with barbed wire and guard dogs. Yet he seems not altogether to have resented them. They protected as well as confined him. The world within them was interesting too as well as safer. Louis greatly relished not only being at sea but also these harassed, beguiling, lushly handsome islands the climate of which met his needs so well. In the most literal sense they gave him insulation.

Until then he had felt little affection for most of the places that he had turned to for health. The first of them, Menton in 1873, when he was twenty-two, led to the ambivalent essay, 'Ordered South' – bleakly frank about the irony of sending alarmed patients to try to get well or at least not die against backgrounds of sunshine, blue water and year-round flowers. Ruefully it notes that 'the places to which we are sent when health deserts us are often singularly

beautiful. Often too . . . places we have visited in former years . . .
we please ourselves with the fancy that we shall repeat many vivid
and pleasurable sensations. . . . I dare say the sick man is not very
inconsolable when he receives sentence of banishment . . . only
after he is settled down [he] begins to understand the change that
has befallen him. . . . Here . . . are the olive gardens and the blue
sea. Nothing can change the eternal magnificence of the naked Alps
behind Mentone . . . [but] of all this [the invalid] has only a cold
head knowledge . . . divorced from enjoyment . . . He is like an
enthusiast leading about with him a stolid, indifferent tourist.
There is someone by who is out of sympathy . . . he seems to touch
things with muffled hands.'³

Louis duly allows for shifts in attitude as weeks pass, and for the
discovery of minor amenities; he sketches at least three other views
of his situation. In such matters it is no good expecting consis-
tency, least of all from young Louis. It is clear, however, that for
this apprentice exile, the Mediterranean's olive groves and wine-
dark sea – *clichés* that should have carried magic – were too much
imbued with the connotations of the sickroom. A decade later he
did find Hyères engaging. The Stevensons lived there in a tiny
pseudo-Swiss cottage built as a model house for the Paris Expo-
sition and moved down to Provence as a landlord's whim. I hope
that its porch still carries the plaque quoting Louis's letter to
Sidney Colvin in which he says: 'I was only happy once; that was at
Hyères.'⁴ Yet the charm of its garden by moonlight could not make
up for the obvious signs that the place did him no good. Davos had
been far worse – brutally black-and-white to look at and artificial
with winter sports and pumped-up doings for the ailing. The deep
snows, dark forests and Arctic temperatures of the Adirondacks
were grimmer still. In Louis Stevenson's mountains there was no
magic, physical or emotional.

I sometimes wonder what he would have made of Thomas
Mann's book. Its variations on the theme of therapeutic exile are
treacherously redolent of the nineteenth-century's sentimentalizing of tuberculosis – a thing certainly familiar to Louis, Keats,
and *La Dame aux Camélias*; and much more to the point, the
wistfully virtuous heroine with a hectic flush in her ivory cheeks
and blood on her lace handkerchief, wasting away, mourned by a
tearfully adoring fiancé and a prayerful family. Actually, of course,
tuberculosis was a major endemic curse to all social strata and
particularly the lowest, so it would be inhumane as well as inaccu-
rate to call the disease fashionable. Yet there was among cultivated

persons an ill-defined, widespread impression that somehow consumption refined and spiritualized its victims, triggered a roman-
tic-flavored sublimation toward higher things. Consonantly the
victim blandly, half-smilingly accepted such necessary depriva-
tions as therapeutic exile. Indeed this talent for cohabiting with the
shadow of death as if it were a becoming scarf round the throat
might be taken as an occasional side-effect of the disease.

And awareness that such behavior was expected may have helped
the exile to manifest it. Experience had already made Louis Stevenson an adept invalid. His illness-racked childhood in a slightly
hypochondriacal family had effected that. Certain traces of this
aesthetic view of his plight appear in his letters and writings. They
are few, however, and mostly early, as if the putative side-effect
soon wore off and left him taking his handicap with mere steady
courage. Or, to give the side-effect notion weight for the sake of
ruling it out in his case, consider the strong possibility that he did
not qualify for the Magic Mountain – that he may not have had
tuberculosis at all. As has been seen, diagnosis was necessarily
mostly educated guessing. Not only was the tubercle bacillus not
yet identified during most of his life, neither X-ray nor tuberculin-
test was yet available. The ablest specialist had little but the stetho-
scope and gross symptoms to work with. America's great Dr Edward Trudeau, one of the first to use bacteriology for diagnosis,
examined Louis at Saranac and decided that if he ever had had
tuberculosis, the case was arrested. And some years ago an American upper respiratory tract specialist studied the scanty data available and suggested that Louis's trouble was not tuberculosis but
chronic severe bronchiectasis – a formidable word meaning heavy
erosion of the bronchial region. That would be consistent with
his sporadic hemorrhages; his childhood history of multiplied
troubles in that area; his tendency to serious infections there in any
but optimum climates and finally with the anomalous fact that at
forty-four he died not of tuberculosis, of which he had shown few
signs for some years, but of a sudden cerebral stroke. If tuberculosis
ever had any romance about it, this finding removes one romantic
detail from the Stevenson story. But it does not vitiate the exile-
therapy. Severe bronchiectasis is just as well advised as tuberculosis to stay in favorable climates.

The major aspect of Stevenson's exile that can be called romantic
– a term I shall not try to define – must still be dealt with. He had a
talent not so much for enforced exile as for the stimulus of dis-
location. As his 'Ordered South' hints, those milder-than-home

climates do have romantic connotations for Northern Europeans; Louis himself noted of one of the German officials infesting Samoa that he had 'that natural love for the tropics which lies so often latent in persons of northern birth'.[5] This is the beakers-full-of-the-warm-South, the *Das-Land-wo-die-Citronen-blühen,* or maybe the best clue is the Briton's or Finn's incredulous delight in the very notion, let alone the actuality, of a palm tree's flourishing outside a greenhouse. Other significant ingredients are water reasonably near skin temperature, sunshine to be counted on more or less daily, and a certain swarthiness in the skins of the local population. Complementary to it all is a still lively tradition of being at sea, particularly under sail.

Stevenson was susceptible to all that. On his 'Ordered South' trip, his first exile, when he opened his shutters in Orange, 'Such a great living flood of sunshine poured in . . . that I confess to having danced and expressed my satisfaction aloud.' And arriving at Menton, walking to his *pension* from the station, 'I was met by a great volley of odors out of the lemon and orange gardens, and . . . I nearly danced again.'[6] Note too that his delight in being at sea by no means depended primarily on overt physical effects. He listed its further advantages as: 'Fine, clean emotions; a world all and always beautiful; air better than wine; interest unflagging; there is upon the whole no better life.'[7] I have known many professional mariners but none who would be as articulately ecstatic, no matter how deeply committed to life on the ocean wave.

Louis once warned his mother that she had a gipsy for a son. Whenever opportunity and health allowed, he demonstrated as much by going on walking tours or paddling a canoe through the French canal system or spending in-and-out weeks in French artists' colonies. The only time in his youth that he had a substantial sum of money, he put much of it into a scheme, with several footloose comrades, to refit a French canal barge as a sort of dormitory studio in which to float in creative peace through all the waterways of Europe. It was to be complete with good cooking, bright paint and geraniums in the stern windows. Her name was to be *The Eleven Thousand Virgins of Cologne.* She never saw service. The syndicate's funds ran out before work was completed and the boatyard sold her for charges. Our point here is that the 'compulsion of circumstances', meaning grave illness, that so often wove the exile thread into Louis's life may have been superfluous.

For there may well also have been a compulsion of temperament. Even had Louis's bellows been as sound as his long legs, the same reckless quirk that nearly drowned him canoeing on the river Oise and sent him navigating a demure donkey through the wilder French mountains might also have sent him to the South Seas. In health as well as illness he had a consistent turn for long absences from home – that is, successive voluntary exiles alternating with short, stimulating but somewhat fidgety returns to Britain. One reason for this pattern was, of course, the chronic strains between himself and Edinburgh, usually personified in his parents. But there again he might have got into that pattern had he been an orphan. Writers are privileged to that sort of life. They can carry their work in their heads and briefcases, and acquaintance with the exotic often provides usably literary material. For a recent instance, W. Somerset Maugham spent decades thus, albeit more luxuriously than was possible for Louis Stevenson.

As for the South Seas – Stevenson's, not Maugham's, they were not at all the same worlds – Louis had a special yearning in that direction. At the age of twenty-four he had spent a long evening with a visiting New Zealander who strongly adjured him, in mouth-watering terms, to take his ailing body to the South Pacific, specifically the Navigator Islands (the old atlas name for Samoa). He recalled thus hearing 'of beautiful places, green forever, perfect shapes of men and women, with red flowers in their hair, and nothing to do but study oratory and etiquette, sit in the sun and pick up the fruits as they fall.'[8] Remark the rapid shift from the therapeutic climate to a Byronic Land of the Doasyoulikes. A few years later when in San Francisco hoping to survive the worst physical crisis he ever knew, and the emotional ordeal of waiting for his wife-to-be's divorce, he frequented seamen's haunts on the Embarcadero. From sailors and other old South Seas hands he heard enticingly about islands with 'precipitous shores, spired mountain tops, the deep shade of hanging forests, the unresting surf upon the reef, and the unending peace of the lagoon; sun, moon and stars of an imperial brightness; man moving in these scenes scarce fallen, and woman lovelier than Eve; the primal curse abrogated, the boat urged, and the long night beguiled with poetry and choral song'.[9] For the complementary sea-going motif, San Francisco Bay showed him much of 'the Island schooner . . . low in the water, with lofty spars and dainty lines, rigged and fashioned like a yacht, manned with brown-skinned, soft-spoken, sweet-eyed native sailors'.[10] There was imminent destiny in the way he reverberated to those elements in the already established notions of the South Seas that become absurd only when stickily overripe. Our suspicion of stereotypes is often carried too far. Proper precaution was recently supplied by a candid sociologist, Nathan Glazer, extolling 'the degree of truth that most stereotypes have, that is, a good deal'.[11]

So one cannot object too harshly to the persistent view of Stevenson as a sort of romantic exile in a stereotype South Seas. Only responsible qualification shrinks the picture almost out of its frame. In a recent book, *A Dream of Islands*,[12] Gavin Daws, an Australian historian of the Pacific area, includes Stevenson as one of five significant nineteenth-century figures associated with the South Seas. The others treated in these biographical studies are Herman Melville; Paul Gauguin; John Williams, a fanatic missionary martyred long before Stevenson's time; and Walter Murray Gibson, a renegade Mormon who, to the eventual detriment of both himself and Hawaii, took his own schizoid delusions seriously. They make an interesting job lot but, once past the prefatory generalities, the author has trouble finding pertinent parallels among them. Indeed about all they had in common was being white, originating outside the area, and spending therein time ranging from a year or so to forty. The grouping is useful, however, in defining Stevenson's special place as South Seas exile. He did not, like Gauguin, verge toward going flabbily native while remaining half beachcomber. Though he came to know and admire certain wholehearted missionaries, he did not, like Williams, approve of tearing out the roots of Polynesian life. He did not, like Gibson, perpetrate swindles to enhance his own power as well as what he took to be the natives' welfare. Nor did he, like Melville – and Gauguin in the other medium – use experience in the area to spread the virulent form of the South Seas obsession that may be called South Seizure.

True, Louis took great pleasure in *Omoo* and *Typee*. The passages that I have just quoted from his own writings carry some of the virus. But even there the topography is actually not overdrawn. I have seen most of the islands that Louis eventually saw and some he did not, and know that foreshore for foreshore, landfall for landfall, just as he promised himself, Polynesia has no superiors and few equals. As to the Polynesians, their winning deference to affluent outsiders and Louis's own habitual good will and imaginative manners made a heady combination. Some of his comments on the more remote Tahitians were rather sticky and he was prone to overplay parallels between Samoan ways and those of Highland clans. For special occasions his Samoan servants, developing a

coherence as of an extended family, wore wraparound skirts of
tartan. It pleased Louis to translate their group-name, 'Tama Ona',
as 'The MacRitchies', for it means 'household of the owner' and in
the Islands 'owner' signified the wealthy and powerful man, the
kind that owns the trading vessel and the trading store. Out of this
genial fiction came something valuable and valid. Louis's Samoan
retainers accorded him a full measure of quasi-feudal honor and
love. But widening acquaintance with high islands and low, Micro-
nesia as well as Polynesia, kept him nearer on course than has ever
been managed by any other creative writer venturing into those
treacherous latitudes.

At first he was rather led up the garden path because his step-
daughter had close ties to Gibson and Hawaiian royalty. His con-
sequent long letter to the London *Times* about Samoa as apple of
discord among three great powers, Germany, Britain and the United
States, showed that as yet he had not visited the actual Samoa. But
out of his subsequent experience there came a sound, detailed
account of the trouble called *A Footnote to History*, treating outside
meddlers with all due scorn yet not sentimentalizing their brown-
skinned victims. His larger book called simply *In the South Seas*,
worked up from his series of newspaper syndicate pieces about the
Islands generally, is still one of the dozen things that a beginning
student thereof must know.

Louis's fictions set in the Islands have the same healthy astrin-
gency and immediacy. He promised, for instance, that his short
novel, *The Beach of Falesá*, would be 'the first realistic South Seas
story . . . with real South Seas characters . . . Everybody else has got
carried away by the romance, and ended in a kind of sham sugar-
candy epic . . . no etching, no human grin, consequently no
conviction. Now I have got the smell and the look of the thing . . .
You will know more about the South Seas after having read my
little tale than if you had read a library.'[13] That uncompromising
pledge was amply redeemed. In another direction the crude cultural
cocktail of the Hawaii of Louis's time begat a short story-fantasy,
'The Isle of Voices', in which Louis's feeling for the supernatural
in Polynesia was free of both the missionary's toploftical rejection
and the enlightened tourist's patronizing interest. The protagonist
is a crassly egocentric young Hawaiian committed to trousers and
tinned salmon from the States. He is both terrified and greedy
when he discovers that his father-in-law is a sorcerer-genie whose
wealth comes from periodic trips on a magic carpet to a faraway
coral atoll where the shells on the beach, properly come at, turn

into new-minted silver dollars. Both the humor and the terror – and the white man's and the brown man's ways – are mixed inextricably, skilfully and effervescently.

Louis's rather ineffective stepson, Lloyd Osbourne, collaborated with him on two novels exploiting South Seas materials, *The Wrecker* and *The Ebb-Tide*. Both show the white man's Pacific as seen from the beach and from the schooner's deck at sea and at anchor in the lagoon and, for all the ambiguities of collaboration, offer highly flavored evidence that Louis's exile was highly formative. For contrast consider Gauguin: give the painter the benefit of every doubt as to why he went to the South Seas, and of every aesthetic merit of the canvases he produced there, it remains true that, to quote myself from thirty-odd years ago: 'The elements in his work usually considered to derive from South Seas background – composition, coloring, emotional impact – are already conspicuous in paintings that he did . . . before he ever saw Tahiti . . . he merely developed against a South Seas set of references the idiom in which he would have painted anywhere.'[14] Randall Jarrell made the same sort of point when saying that T. S. Eliot would have written *The Waste Land* about the Garden of Eden. Whereas close acquaintance with Stevenson's work shows that much he did after settling in Samoa has dimensions and textures that he had never attained before, indeed had seldom sought. The crowning demonstration is, of course, *Weir of Hermiston,* the novel he was working on when he died. Its atmosphere was utterly Scottish, no hint of the South Seas. But it is a general maturing that develops here regardless of what specific materials are handled.

The simple explanation is that mere time was maturing his skills and insights. It is conceivable that had he never left Scotland, his talent would have expanded up to the *Weir of Hermiston* level. But here the scientist's elegant preference for the simple accounting is probably unsound. Had Louis never left Scotland, he might well never have survived to write his later works. And since writing does to some extent depend on well being, the new dimensions of what he did at Vailima might never have evolved for lack of the requisite underlying physical tone. Somewhere Goethe said that no man knows his own language until he is well acquainted with another. True, certain admitted giants like Shakespeare and Homer – and Mother Goose, if you like – dazzle posterity without ever getting outside their cultural matrix. But how fortunate it was that Milton had those formative experiences in Italy! Stevenson was not unaware of cross-cultural stimuli. While exploring the island of

Tutuila one Sunday he hears a church bell ring: 'How many different stories are told by that drum of tempered iron! To the natives, a
strange, outlandish new theory; to us of Europe, redolent of home;
in the ears of the [missionary] priests calling up memories of
French and Flemish cities, and perhaps some carved cathedral, and
the pomp of celebrations; in mine, talking of the grey metropolis of
the north, of a certain village on a certain stream, of remote chur-
ches, rustic congregations, and of vanished faces and silent
tongues.'[15] Geneticists speak of a 'hybrid vigor', meaning that
sometimes the crossing of two varieties produces in certain con-
sequent individuals a plant or animal larger or stronger than either
parent. If not overworked the analogy can be useful here. One can
insist that this was a matter merely of Stevenson's being forced to
resort to the South Seas, toward which romanticized accounts
inclined him anyway, just when time and biochemistry were bringing him maturity as a writer. But I prefer the more dynamic reading:
that his half-forced, half-voluntary exile afforded him not only
physical benefits but also immersed him in environmental and
crosscultural impingements that did much to jar his talent into
maturity. The second is reinforced by the consideration that beginning in Hawaii, he embarked on a highly positive political activity.

Professor Harvie has given a most knowledgeable account of
Stevenson's political attitudes in the context of the Europe he
knew. The ingenious use of *Prince Otto* as pertinent datum particularly struck me; it was my first glimpse of what that work's
excuse for existence might be. The other data were also impressively marshalled. In partial disagreement, however, I have difficulty regarding Louis as a significantly political animal until he
reached the South Seas. The phase of articulate Unionism that he
manifested in the 1880s seems to me to some extent another of the
deviations from his natural orbit that William Ernest Henley's
gravitational pull brought about. Hence it lacked the organic meaning of his political activity in Samoa. Note too that early in his
career Louis had recognized the likelihood of such shifts from
impatiently liberal youth to conservative middle age in a cheeky
essay, 'Crabbed Age and Youth', in which when Age says to Youth:
'Ah, so I thought when I was your age', Youth retorts: 'My venerable sir, so I shall most probably think when I am yours'.[16] His
Unionism I see as dabbling in contrast to the deeper commitments
of his South Seas years.

Those indignant letters to *The Times* were self-inspired efforts
to influence home opinion toward a greater sense of responsibility

toward the Islands. *A Footnote to History* had the same purpose. The laird of Vailima soon found his sympathies and new-hatched political impulses enlisting him as supporter of Mataafa, the likeliest of the three native faction-leaders struggling for hegemony of Samoa – a parochial squabble bedevilled by the cynicism, opportunism and inconsistent negligence of the great powers. Stevenson visited Mataafa in his rebel camp and was received with the ceremony due a powerful ally. The occasion was the more notable because, with a larkishness as characteristic as it was ill advised, he once brought with him a vivacious lady visitor to Samoa, the Countess of Jersey – whose husband happened to be the incumbent Crown governor of New South Wales. Presently the comic opera tripartite government imprisoned Mataafa's chief followers, and Stevenson and his family ostentatiously took them elaborate aid and comfort. Behind such gestures it was locally important that the prestige of Vailima weighed heavy in Mataafa's pan of the scales. Thirty years ago I was a grateful guest at Vailima for two months, when it was the residence of the Commissioner administering Western Samoa for New Zealand. His hospitality was warm in the Stevenson tradition. But I must describe the establishment as a commodious, comfortable sort of refined barracks suitable to the climate. It can hardly have been palatial even when housing Stevenson books, silver and furniture brought from Scotland. To the Samoan mind, however, it was a palace of wonder and magic and it followed that its Ona was a figure to conjure with. Hence Thurston's temptation to order Stevenson deported. The upshot of it all was that, some years after Louis died, Germany got the lion's share of Samoa and the United States the strategically useful harbor of Pagopago in Tutuila.

From the perspective of almost ninety years Stevenson's heightened energies in that sordid context seems a symptom of a general shift of emotional base with a growingly paradoxical effect on his choice of subjects to write about. The more he felt responsibly involved in his island life, the better he understood that he would never venture home again; or was it the other way round? Anyway the situation seems to have sharpened his sense of exile. Some of his late letters and verses express it poignantly, as several of my colleagues have pointed out, and a subtle extension of it gradually nudged him away from South Seas materials toward others brimming up from his earlier years. The frames of reference were not altogether Scottish. At his death he left, barely begun, several novels that, had he had another ten years, might have been remark-

able. They drew on Revolutionary France, Regency England. . . .
One of the best opens in Avignon with the *mistral* blustering
outside and a turbulent, hulking wineshop-keeper looming
jealously over his beautiful and accessible wife in a composition
that Daumier might have painted. But note that after a few pages
Scotland enters in the shape of a noble follower of fugitive Charles
Stuart; and then the fugitive himself. Another opening almost as
brilliant is altogether Scottish – a few thousand words about an
adolescent boy running dangerous errands for the Covenanters.
Scotland was, of course, the chief setting for *Catriona,* the sequel
to *Kidnapped* completed at this period. The early chapters of *St
Ives,* the energetic semi-potboiler four-fifths completed at Louis's
death, are full of Edinburgh and the drove roads very lovingly
treated. And *Weir of Hermiston* is solidly Scottish.

David Daiches's recent short biography ably celebrates how
much Stevenson owed to his sense of topography as catalyst for
emotion. Doubtless that faculty was one thing sharpening his
sense of exile in the final years. 'Here I am until I die, and there will
I be buried', he wrote to S.R.Crockett eighteen months before the
end. 'The word is out and the doom written.'[17] Impulsively one
wishes that it had not been so, that he could have seen the Castle
Rock again. But the second impulse is to suspect that he may have
been better off, given all the circumstances, with the insubstantial
Scotland imprinted on his brain cells, clarified and refined to its
essential lines, like a good drawing, by his powerful sense of
topography and atmosphere. A return of any duration risked a
cluttering up with details and petty memories of the statelier,
grayer, gaunter, windier Edinburgh that, in certain emotional
weathers, he saw out of his workroom window overlooking the
Pacific. It would be unforgiveably coldblooded to regard his exile as
a prescription from Dr Pangloss of the best thing for him, per-
sonally and professionally as well as physically. The element of
compulsion rules out any such objectivity. But it does remain
likely that he owed to the hybrid vigor of exile things that he might
otherwise never have achieved.

References
Unless otherwise stated, from South Seas edition,
Charles Scribner's Sons, New York 1925.
1 'Ordered South', Nottingham Society ed.
  (New York, n.d.) VI, 216.
2 *The Wrecker,* XXI, 289-90.
3 'Ordered South', Nottingham Society ed., VI, 215.

4　*Letters* III, XXI, 249.
5　*A Footnote to History*, XXVI, 173.
6　To Mrs Sitwell, *Letters* I, XXIX, 117-18.
7　To Sidney Colvin, *Letters* III, XXXI, 114.
8　To Mrs Sitwell, *Letters* I, XXIX, 269.
9　*The Wrecker*, XXI, 130.
10　ibid., 123.
11　Nathan Glazer and Daniel P. Moynihan, *Beyond the Melting Pot*, second edition, MIT Press [1970], 33.
12　New York, W. W. Norton, 1980.
13　To Sidney Colvin, *Letters* III, XXXI, 292.
14　J. C. Furnas, *Anatomy of Paradise* (London, Victor Gollancz 1950) 426-7.
15　'Tutuila', *Vailima Papers*, XXVI, 49.
16　'Crabbed Age and Youth', Nottingham Soc. ed., VI, 193.
17　To S. R. Crockett, *Letters* IV, XXXII, 178.

Notes on Contributors

DAVID DAICHES

Professor of English at Sussex University until 1977; author of *Robert Louis Stevenson* (1947) and *Robert Louis Stevenson and His World* (1973).

MICHAEL BALFOUR

Professor of European Studies at the University of East Anglia until 1974; son of Graham Balfour, Stevenson's cousin and his first authorised biographer.

TREVOR ROYLE

Freelance writer; author of *Precipitous City* (1980), a literary history of Edinburgh.

DOUGLAS GIFFORD

Lecturer in the Department of English Studies at the University of Strathclyde; has published articles on Scottish literature.

W.W.ROBSON

Masson Professor of English Literature at the University of Edinburgh; has published articles on *Treasure Island*.

CHRISTOPHER HARVIE

Professor of British Studies at the University of Tübingen; author of *The Lights of Liberalism* (1976) and *Scotland and Nationalism* (1977).

J.C.FURNAS

Freelance writer and journalist in the United States; author of *Voyage to Windward* (1952), an unrivalled biography of Stevenson.

JENNI CALDER

Author of *RLS: A Life Study* (1980) and editor of *A Robert Louis Stevenson Companion* (1980); general editor of a new collected edition of Stevenson's works.